Diana,

Love & Blessings

Courtney Hall

xo

AWAKEN

Visionary Insight
PRESS

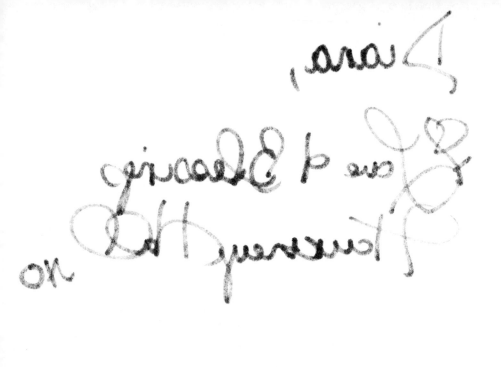

AWAKEN

AWAKEN

Ordering information: Quantity Sales. Special discounts are available on quantity purchases by corporations, associations, and others. For details, contact the "Special Sales Department at Visionary Insight Press."

Visionary Insight Press, 822 Westchester Place, Charleston, IL 61920

Visionary Insight Press, the Visionary Insight Press logo and its individual parts are trademarks of Visionary Insight Press.

Compiled by: Lisa Hardwick-Peplow
Editor-At-Large: Chelle Thompson
Back cover photo credit: Shannon Ridge Photography/Boulder Colorado, Stephanie Michelle Photography, Andrea Hillebrand, Henry Roy Photography, Michael Duhe, Zach Sutton Photography, Mona Lisa Cook, Addison A. Cumberbatch–Studio: Willie Alleyne Associates, Captured Moments Photography, Dan Skaramuca, dba Contempo Studio, Tina Lay Photography, Nicole Ryan Photography, Patricia Holdsworth Photography, Jenny Paul, NCL Photography, Kendal Vaughan Photography, Tracey Photography, Dustin Cook

The First Notes

"hearing the first notes inside
herself, her eyes got wide. growing
louder and stronger, colors began
mixing with the sounds. holding
on tight and letting go all at once,
she stepped back into the dance."

~ TERRI ST. CLOUD
www.BoneSighArts.com

Table of Contents

"Carefully listen to the whisper of your heart. It's there to guide you."

~ INGRID COOK

Foreword

by Chelle Thompson

🌀 "Without change, something sleeps inside us, and seldom awakens. The sleeper must AWAKEN."

~ FRANK HERBERT

Have you ever had a wake-up call that brought your whole world into focus ... one that jolted you out of your comfort zone? I now know that those unexpected challenges are meant to deliver evolutionary options. They are the awakening trumpets that herald crossroad opportunities for us to expand our consciousness and "lean in" to our Higher Good.

I've experienced so many predicaments that looked like disasters, yet they eventually revealed themselves as incredible gifts and pivotal turning points. It took me decades to fully embrace the fact that difficulties were actually doorways — I just needed to awaken to the signals, step through and take action. While it may seem almost impossible, we humans can actually choose to awaken and change everything.

Motivational author and speaker, Jim Rohn states, "Any day we wish, we can start the process of life change. We can do it immediately, or next week, or next month, or next year. We can also do NOTHING. We can pretend rather than perform. And if the idea of having to change ourselves makes us uncomfortable, we can remain as we are. We can choose rest over labor, entertainment over education, delusion over truth, and doubt over confidence. The choices are ours to make. But while we curse the effect, we continue to nourish the cause. As Shakespeare uniquely observed, '*The fault is not in the stars, but in ourselves.*' We created our circumstances by our past choices. We have both the ability and the responsibility to make better choices beginning today."

Although we may not see it initially, the struggles created by our past choices are often exactly what our soul requires — for if we were to operate without obstacles, our wings would not grow as strong and we might not believe we can fly. It's equally important that we do not let old judgment errors keep us glued to an unhealthy path. When we release yesterday and embrace the present, we are setting the stage to love ourselves and recognize our intrinsic worth.

The courageous women authors in this book were all awakened by significant events in their lives and wisely chose to empower themselves by making changes. The process was never easy, yet it expedited their blossoming into radiant beings here on Earth. Several of the ladies had occurrences of Angelic Intervention which shifted their perspectives or even saved them from peril. They arose, dusted themselves off and made new choices that brought them inner peace and joy. These women then wrote about their transformational incidents from a place of deep gratitude.

Gratitude is the key to long-lasting bliss and fulfillment. The more we bless those magical moments that brightened our existence, the more they'll feel 'invited' to return ... because, sometimes, even guardian angels need a *green light!*

CHELLE THOMPSON is an Author, Poet, Minister of Conscious Studies and Editor-Publisher of Inspiration Line. She has an extensive background in recovery programs, motivational counseling, psychology and theology. Inspiration Line's Meaningful Life website and global e-magazine reach more than 235 countries worldwide. Chelle's skills in international travel writing and human relations provide this project with an insightful and diversified foundation. In 1991, Chelle left a successful advertising career in Southern California and followed her Inner Voice to New Mexico, where she knew no one. In Santa Fe, she established a holistic center and published a monthly magazine that was distributed nationally.

www.InspirationLine.com
Chelle@InspirationLine.com

Michelle Mullady

MICHELLE MULLADY is a Joyful Living Mentor, Master Energy Intuitive, Spiritual Guide, Author, and Transformational Healing Workshop Leader who specializes in clairvoyance, clairaudience, clairsentience, and spirit realm communication. She is able to elevate the frequency of emotional, mental and physical bodies. She is here to help you heal from the past so that you can live vibrantly in the present moment. She is here to teach you how to reconnect with and use your intuitive sixth sense as a guiding force in your personal world. It is her passion to help you discover and fall in love with your brilliant and authentic inner self.

info@MichelleMullady.com
www.MichelleMullady.com

Life Is About Who You Love, So Love Yourself

🌀 "I allow myself to experience love."

Each morning I take about five minutes to stand in front of a mirror and lovingly look into my own eyes, as I say to myself out loud, *"I love and approve of you. You are beautiful and wonderful exactly as you are. You are worthy and deserving of love. I love being you!"*

For many years I lived with a guarded heart. I desperately avoided my true feelings and the issues I'd acquired throughout my life. My patterns of self-hatred began long ago in an addictive childhood environment where I suffered mental, emotional, physical, and sexual abuse as a "normal" lifestyle. Being starved for love, nurturance and affection in healthy ways, I did not know how to extend love and kindness to myself, because it was not taught or expressed clearly and consistently in my formative years. Therefore, I found myself attracted to other dysfunctional families, friends, boyfriends, and work situations which only continued to reaffirm my core beliefs that I was unlovable, valueless, and of no importance to the world. I also carried a spiritual belief that I was a sinner who was being punished by God.

Needless to say, I felt isolated, alone, terrified, and depressed from one day to the next. I developed many ways of coping through self-abusive addictions to food, excessive exercise, drama and chaos, painful relationships, shopping, creating debt, and over the top use of drugs and alcohol in an attempt to fill my heartbreak and self-loathing wounds. Life was far from happy and I lived in a world made up of my own mental and emotional hell.

Then, one day my soul just opened up. In my early twenties my life began changing in big ways. I finally hit my emotional bottom and something deep inside me told me that I could no longer go on existing in the out-of-control lifestyle that I had manifested through my inner turmoil.

I felt a longing for peace that I had never known and a desire for unconditional love and authentic joy that welled up inside of me like a fountain. I wanted to be set free from my prison. I was ready to begin the journey of healing my life and learning to love myself. Although on a conscious level, I was completely unaware of what an awe-inspiring path this would be.

But, I didn't love myself overnight. It took some serious dedication to change on my part. I had to become willing to, one day at a time, show up for my inner journey and learn to have an improved relationship with myself. As I grew to love all of who I am, my world started budding in beautiful and mysterious ways. My heart has softened and opened wide to receiving and giving love and I now see through very different eyes. My pledge to follow this calling expanded, and in the process, Divine Love made itself known by leading my life. I believe this ever-present source and supply is the miracle of universal unconditional love that is available to us all.

Over the past two decades I have been learning to recognize and accept this gift. Cultivating love and compassion for myself made it possible.

Why Learning to Love Yourself is Beneficial

🌀 "I love and accept myself as a unique individual."

Learning to love yourself is the quantum leap forward that can make every area of your life better. I have even come to know that learning to love yourself is the key movement from which mental, emotional, physical and spiritual health flows. It is the most powerful, therapeutic technique I know of and I use it for my own evolution. It is the central part of living a peaceful and blissful life. I am continually being moved and inspired by the power of self-love to transform the lives of individuals in my work with men and women from around the world. Whether I am seeing private clients, leading a group, or teaching a workshop, time and again I have witnessed that people learning to love themselves often causes depressions to lift, relationships to improve, and even longstanding physical illnesses to disappear. If you could only do one thing for your well-being, I would appeal to you to learn to love yourself from the inside out.

Many of the individuals I have been blessed to support on their journey to the heart, however, have found it difficult to allow themselves the time needed to begin these changes. In truth, I found that most people find the idea of loving themselves to be attached to limiting societal and spiritual beliefs that state that it is an act of vanity and self-centeredness. They fear the loss of love and approval from others if they begin to develop self-love. As a result of these mindset limitations, most people wait until the last possible moment before learning to love themselves. They knock at my door consumed with self-loathing, poor health, low self-esteem, their relationships in ruins, financial issues, spiritual disconnection, emotional turmoil, and their life purpose completely out of focus and unclear. Far too many people make the transition from this reality to the next without ever discovering the joy of loving themselves. Does it have to be this way? I certainly don't think so from my experience—especially with all of the self-help resources that we have available in abundance in this day and age. Self-love is a growing possibility for every soul.

People who sincerely love themselves do not become destructively self-absorbed. They do not mistreat others. They do not stop growing and changing. People who love themselves well, learn to love others skillfully too. They continually develop into healthier people, wisely understanding that their love was properly placed. Therefore, when you begin your journey you are initiating a ripple effect that can flow around the globe.

Awakening to Self-Love

"I deserve my own praise, appreciation, and self-care. I am willing to commit to giving myself the love that I know that I am worth. I allow myself to be loved. I am responsible for my experience. I am choosing to love and approve of myself. I see myself with the eyes of love, and I am safe."

In the realm of self-love, a little bit can go a long way. I promise that you will be surprised at how tiny a door you will have to open in order to invite in the transformational power of love. Grant yourself permission, in the here and now, to awaken to love, so that you can go on to fulfill your potential in this lifetime.

For most of you, truly learning to love yourself seems so elusive, much more work than you expected. For myself it was a process that became a daily practice of developing new habits that required my affectionate attention. I had to identify, undo and relearn a lifetime of unhealthy patterns and behaviors by replacing them with fresh options. Giving myself the time and attention I had so desperately wanted from others all my life has been, in itself, my most profound act of self-love.

I have learned more from my own self-care than from anyone else that I am lovable, I do matter, my life is valuable and extremely important. I have had many teachers, but ultimately it was my own commitment to loving myself that created the results that I longed for.

I have made the analogy that if you keep giving to others without giving to yourself it is like pouring water from a vessel. If you pour without ever refilling it, eventually, the vessel will inevitably run dry. If you are the vessel, how do you refill, recharge, re-energize, and replenish yourself, so that you will have love to give to others and the world? The answer is by loving and giving to yourself first. How do you begin this?

Let's start with some practical suggestions on how to chart a new path towards connecting even more deeply with yourself. Allow me to be your guide to awaking your self-love.

🌟 "Let the Light of Love nourish yourself.
Believe in who you are. And you will see
yourself blossom like a beautiful flower."

~ KIRAN SHAIKH

Journey to the Heart

🌟 "I open my mind and heart to miracles."

You are undoubtedly stepping outside your comfort zone by considering the possibility of loving yourself. If you're ready, you can start today. The first step is to be willing. With the slightest willingness, you will receive Divine guidance to move forward. I invite you to begin practicing the idea right now, in this instant, by repeatedly affirming to yourself, ***I am worthy and deserving of my own love.*** For the next twenty-one days, recite this affirmation. Say it over and over to yourself as a miracle mantra. Post it on your wall, your mirror and anywhere that you feel inspired to place it where you will see it throughout your day. Put it everywhere. Make a daily commitment to be willing to love yourself. By simply setting this intention, you are one step closer to loving yourself.

Then, congratulate yourself for having the courage to grow. Your willingness to evolve to a higher level of consciousness will certainly touch the lives of many people. May you continue to awaken to the love that is your birthright to enjoy.

Eleven 'Love Yourself' Tools

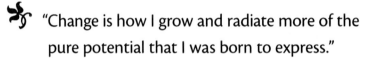 "Change is how I grow and radiate more of the pure potential that I was born to express."

There are many options for loving and caring for yourself—the possibilities are infinite. The following eleven 'Love Yourself' tools have worked for me and countless others who I have guided over my many years in private practice. Each person creates a unique pattern to incorporate these tools into their own lives. I welcome you to do the same.

◌ 1. Support Yourself with Healthy Guidance

You were not meant to walk this journey alone, especially in your time of need. So the very first step towards loving yourself is seeking guidance and support from other individuals who are on the same path and perhaps farther along than you are at this time. In other words ... FIND YOUR TRIBE ... those people who are walking the self-love talk. Help can come in the form of an individual practitioner, a small support group, a large community, or all of the above.

These Earth Angels will continuously be there, sending you supportive and healing energy and awaiting your requests for help as you tumble, and rejoice with you in your triumphs.

Ask, and listen in the stillness to the Universe for guidance, which shows up as signs to steer you to the people who can best assist you in this present moment.

☙ 2. Honesty is Clarity

Make a searching and fearless inventory of yourself to get clear about how you've been unloving towards yourself. Are you possibly drinking too much, hooked on drugs (even prescription medication), overeating, staying in bad relationships, reciting negative mantras in your head? Make a list of all the ways you mistreat yourself. Carefully and kindly, look at the list and ask, "Would I treat someone I love that way?" Make this a tool. Each time you treat yourself badly with your thoughts and actions, ask yourself that question. By continuing to take a personal inventory and admitting you are wrongly hurting yourself, you witness your negative behavior and stop identifying with it. Then, choose some new way to love yourself to replace it and create a new moment. In the instant that you choose self-love over negativity, you create a shift and get one step closer to truly loving who you are.

☙ 3. Create a Daily Self-Love 'Can Do' List

Write or type out a list on a piece of paper of everything agreeable and desirable that you can do to love yourself daily. Carry it around with you as a reminder of the choices that you can make to honor and care for yourself when you're craving to repeat unhealthy patterns arises again.

Here is an example of my list:

Notice your thoughts, take conscious deep breaths when you are feeling stressed, feel all of your feelings, say I AM … I am loving, lovable, and loved, look for the positive, relax, meditate, pray, and express gratitude frequently.

🌟 For a printable FREE GIFT version of this list go to
http://www.michellemullady.com/free-gifts.html
to download and print your copy.

❧ 4. Feel and Heal All of Your Feelings

Emotional energy is an integral part of being human. Your feelings are vast and powerful, like rays of the sun, they desire to be dispelled *outwardly*. You need to acknowledge your emotions and find new positive ways to express them. Pent-up and outdated, old unprocessed feelings clog your ability to fully experience the joy, peace, and devotion that you have been yearning for, as well as create physical conditions of dis-ease in the body, so begin to make friends with your emotions today.

When you release the stale emotional energy of the past and the false beliefs linked to it, your spirit ignites and your body shifts. You experience a cleansing and detoxification. Transformation takes place on several levels. In time a new lesson comes to light. You awaken to the truth that you can choose happiness, freedom, forgiveness, and self-love.

❧ 5. Keep a Journal

Journaling is a helpful tool that can heal, enhance, and nourish your well-being. Through keeping a daily, weekly, or monthly journal you can communicate your physical feelings, clear the deep lake fed by the river of your emotions, record your thoughts and experiences, turn negatives into positives, give your imagination free rein, clear away clutter, articulate yourself in creative ways, connect with your inner child, and stretch yourself beyond your believed limitations. By making this activity an important part of your process you will become intimately acquainted with all of your diverse interior aspects, which has an overall effect of encouraging you to arrive at new heights. The process of writing opens you up to receiving new ideas and information. You tap into your soul's energy, as well as the wisdom of the universe.

☙ 6. Say Loving, Encouraging, and Healing Statements to Yourself Every Day.

Oh, I just love this one. As you awaken, one of the most potent processes you will go through is re-parenting yourself, forgiving your family of origin and choosing your new inner dialogue. Nurture yourself with positive and supportive self-talk, because your soul flourishes on praise and compliments. Frequently tell yourself, "I love you," either silently or out loud. It is such a powerful action that aligns you with the law of attraction and centers you in a LOVE VORTEX. Try out this "Affirmation Bath":

Take a moment to relax and BREATHE. Breathing in through your nose and breathing out through your mouth. Giggle. Give yourself a HUGE hug. Say: *"With an open heart and mind I welcome a wonderful life."* Smile. Breathing in say: *"I know that I deserve a wonderful life."* Breathe. Say: *"I willingly accept the highest and the best in my life now."* With another deep breath say: *"I am an incredible person, worthy of a great life, and I lovingly approve of myself. I love you, _____. I truly love who you are in every moment. You are my dearest friend. I am looking forward to walking the journey of a lifetime with you. I know that each day my life will continue to get better and better."* Breathe. *"My love for you is constant. I know that with you I will experience many enjoyable adventures and each step of the way I will move forward on my path to loving myself."*

☙ 7. Pamper Yourself

You deserve to receive wonderful treatment, extra-special care, grand gifts, and other forms of pampering from your experience. Work on joyously giving and accepting the bounties in your life. Find healthy ways to nurture your mind, body, emotions, and spirit.

Indulge yourself with a nap, a massage, eat good food, laze around in nature, listen to elevating music, light some candles, take a hot lavender Epsom salt bath, or go play at a park. Value your wants and needs. Discover what makes you feel happy and do it often.

✎ 8. Pray Affirmatively

Develop a true spiritual practice by re-forming the words you use in prayer to empower you to realize your own True identity, and then claim it and live it.

 "Dear Spirit, I am in love with allowing you to love me. I am saying "YES" to life in new and surprising ways. I am trusting the grand Plan to be better than anything I have ever imagined. I am floating in the Heavens of my Higher Self and basking in the beauty of the Universal Love flowing through me now. And so it is ... Amen."

✎ 9. Meditate

Use daily meditation as an effortless act of self-love. Approach this practice with ease and as a joyous escape in whatever way feels most comfortable and natural to you. Try it sitting and laying down. Always begin with several conscious deep breaths. Let go of rules or guidelines and give your mind permission to quiet itself at its own pace. Compassionately allow your body to slow down in its own harmony. It's intended to be a time when your mind is completely connected to your heavenly home where you're filled with energy, ideas, and tranquility.

❧ View my 'I AM LOVE' video meditation to
help you increase and strengthen your core
self-love at http://www.michellemullady.com/

❀ 10. Send Love to Your Heart

Your entire being responds positively to love. When you express this energy towards your physical self, it has the same effect as if it was sent to you by someone else. Love is love, no matter what channel it streams through.

Take some time now to sit in your sacred place. Begin to feel the energy held within. Place your right hand over your heart center and speak these words aloud:

❧ "I breathe in love, and I flow with life. I surround
myself with the astonishing pink light of the
universe. May this healing light of unconditional
love enter every area of my reality and fill my
heart and soul. May the magic of love always
move me to radiate warmth and caring to
myself and all those who touch my life."

❀ 11. Spend Time Alone

Become comfortable with being alone. This tool will assist you in developing a more meaningful relationship with your inner self. Once a day, spend at least ten minutes of quiet time unaccompanied. Turn off your cell phone, stop tweeting and texting, and start seeking serenity. Listen to your thoughts and check in with your body. Simply slow down enough to become aware of the loving voice of your inner guide and what it is saying to you.

Trust the Process

🌀 "I am in love with loving me."

External love manifests as an expression of your inner love. Center your energy there, center your attention there, focus on building your own luminous interior 'Love Field', healing your heart, opening to the universal heart and on falling in love with YOU.

You cannot truly give or receive love if you do not love yourself. The path of your soul's evolution in this lifetime is learning to love yourself. Trust the process, be patient and LOVE YOURSELF first.

Dedicated to the creative force of divine unconditional love in this universe, and the Creator. I wrote this for people on the path to discovering passionate self-love. May you remember your magnificence and share your Self with the world.

To all of my devoted clients from around the world, my delightful friends and awe-inspiring mentors and teachers—I am filled to overflowing with the dazzling light of your souls. A special thank you to my two joyful boys, Ibán and Lucio, and my mega supportive life partner, Mauricio. You are the reason I strive daily to AWAKEN and ride the energy flow. You make my life colorful with LOVE.

~Michelle Mullady

Valentina Galante

VALENTINA GALANTE is a Certified Heal Your Life® Workshop Leader, Life Coach, and Founder of KickAssJoy™. She is dedicated to using her inner peace, compassion, and insight to inspire and guide people to experience their own inner peace and kick-ass joy in a world where everyone loves themselves and each other unconditionally.

She and her two daughters live in Bradenton, Florida, where they enjoy going to the beach, wearing their mermaid tails, and discovering new ways to have FUN!

athomeValentina@aol.com
www.kickassjoy.com

 The Art of Noise

S ound: "the sensation produced by stimulation of the organs of hearing by vibrations transmitted through the air or other medium".

Aaaaahhhhh, my children's laughter, a babbling brook, birds chirping to greet the day, a beautiful melody ... these are just some of my favorite sounds. As a person blessed with a high sensitivity to what I hear, I've always noticed the sounds around me, and have paid close attention to how they make me feel. Sound is vibration, like everything else in the Universe, so it naturally follows that it would have a great influence on our well-being. When we perceive it as pleasant, it affects us in positive ways, and when it becomes excessive, or discordant, it becomes noise and can affect us negatively.

I remember a time, years ago, when I was an International Flight Attendant with a major airline, had a home-based business, was stuck in an unhappy marriage, was experiencing other family issues, had two wonderful, but very energetic daughters to take care of, and was not managing my stress very well. I became hypersensitive to all sounds, including the ones I used to love, was anxious all the time, and was completely overwhelmed. I eventually developed health issues so severe that my life came to a screeching halt. I was scared, and didn't know if I'd ever have a normal life again. I knew I had to make some changes.

During that time, I was introduced to a book by Louise L. Hay called *You Can Heal Your Life*. This book changed my life! I learned, among other things, that I was co-creating my reality with my thoughts, words and focus. I learned that thoughts, like sound, have a vibration, and they become "noise" in our head when they are negative, excessive, or obsessive. They can contribute greatly to our stress levels. I learned that specific thoughts could affect specific areas of the body. For instance, people who have lower back issues often have worries about the future and about money. Louise's book includes a huge list of physical ailments, their probable causes, and the suggested new thought patterns to help heal that area of the body.

I became fascinated with learning more about the mind/body connection and even started seeing a biofeedback therapist. My therapist hooked me up to monitors that measured my skin temperature, muscle tension, and brainwave activity. I was able to see on the monitors how my thoughts affected my body, and that when I changed my thought patterns, it had a very positive, or healing effect on me. It was strong proof for me that if I changed my thoughts, and that if I quieted the negative mind chatter, I could change my life.

My transformation was quite dramatic once I learned this information! I was eventually able to completely turn my life around. My body now feels wonderful, I love my life, and am finally able to feel real joy in a way in which I never had before. I became so passionate about helping those in emotional pain turn their lives around as well, that I became a Certified Heal Your Life® workshop leader and life coach in the philosophy of Louise Hay. What follows are just a few of the many tools I used to quiet both the inner noise and external noise in my life that helped me heal, and that I now use to help others to access their own inner peace and happiness too.

Pay Attention to Your Thoughts

🌀 "Be the silent watcher of your thoughts and behavior. You are beneath the thinker. You are the stillness beneath the mental noise. You are the love and joy beneath the pain."

~ ECKHART TOLLE

This was a *really* big one for me. The Law of Attraction states that what we focus on expands. One reason I had been so stressed-out was because for many years I kept focusing on what *wasn't* working in my life. I was continually focused on my frustration about it. It just seemed to be automatic. I would obsess about things that had occurred, would talk about it often and would worry about things that might happen in the future, without realizing that doing so caused me more stress and that it attracted more negative experiences to me. I was in a contracted, fear-based energy or vibration. When I finally learned to pay attention to those thoughts and learned how to turn them around, everything changed.

Whenever I caught myself worrying or complaining during those early days, I would say "STOP, Valentina!" "What are you thinking about?" This exercise was *extremely* helpful in allowing me to realize exactly where I needed to make changes in my thinking. I then would focus instead on what I wanted to *create* in my life, what I was grateful for, and on using positive affirmations. To this day, if I'm feeling stressed I ask that same question, and then consciously turn my thinking around. I now say many positive affirmations daily, which helps keep me in that positive space. I now feel like I'm in the flow of life, and good things are happening every day. It feels great!

Our *perception* about events has a tremendous impact on our inner peace and happiness, as well. My mentor, Marci Shimoff, author, featured teacher in the movie *The Secret*, and happiness expert, encourages us to look at the "gifts and the lessons" in every situation. Although doing so is not always easy, it *can* be incredibly rewarding. *Every* time I do this when it comes to a difficult situation in my life, or when I think about something that has happened in my past, I learn from it, gain valuable insight, and feel more peaceful. It quiets that negative mind chatter. Marci Shimoff has also taught me to ask, "If this were happening for a bigger purpose, for my soul's growth, what would that be?" We can learn from every situation, and when we are able to slow down and look at the bigger picture, it can bring great clarity, understanding, and calm. We may not always have control over what happens in life, but we always have control over how we look at it.

Self-Love

> "Loving yourself is the most important thing you can do, because when you love yourself, you are not going to hurt yourself or anyone else. It's the prescription for world peace."
>
> ~ LOUISE L. HAY

Sometimes we are our own worst critics. I know I was. Through reading *You Can Heal Your Life* by Louise L. Hay, I learned the importance of loving myself. It was a *huge* game-changer for me. I started to pay attention to some of the ways in which I would criticize myself, and gradually stopped saying anything negative about myself, even jokingly. When I learned how to quiet my inner critic, it was incredibly healing.

When I was going through my divorce, I would look at myself in the mirror, and say nice, kind, loving things to myself ... out loud! It's what helped me get through that emotionally-challenging time. Whenever I felt down, I would just talk to myself and praise myself for what I was doing right, for being strong, for being loving to my two daughters, and for persevering. My kids probably thought I was "coo-coo", but that's okay. For those of you with teenagers, you know that's kind of par for the course anyway, right? When we love ourselves, we also set a great example for our children. So many kids—especially adolescents—feel insecure, and don't feel "good enough" compared to others. When we can send them out into the world knowing their worth, they will also reach for all the good the Universe has to offer.

If it sounds strange to talk to yourself in the mirror, just imagine what you might say to your best friend in that situation, or to your 5-year-old self. Then look at yourself in the mirror and say one positive thing. That's a good start. Start by doing it every morning and you'll see that it becomes easier and easier.

Ultimately we're the only person we're guaranteed to be with from the first day of our lives, until the last day. Doesn't it make sense, then, to create the most harmonious, positive, and loving relationship with ourselves? Doesn't it make sense, then, to be our own best friend? When we treat ourselves with love, we go into the world in a more peaceful way. When we love ourselves, we won't put up with being in dysfunctional relationships, we don't stay in jobs where we're not appreciated, and we don't mistreat our bodies. Instead, we reach for quality in our lives because we feel deserving of all the good the Universe has for us, not in an arrogant way, but in a grateful way. It keeps us in an expanded energy which brings more happiness and joy into our lives.

Get rid of the drama!

🌀 "There comes a time in your life, when you walk away from all the drama and people who create it. You surround yourself with people who make you laugh. Forget the bad, and focus on the good. Love the people who treat you right, pray for the ones who don't."

~ JOSE N. HARRIS

Drama in our relationships causes both inner and outer noise that affects us in many ways. In her book, *Happy for No Reason*, Marci Shimoff shares that "our relationships have a biochemical effect on our bodies. When we make healthy connections with people, our brains flood our cells with happiness chemicals, and when we have unhealthy social interactions, harmful chemicals are released." She also cites a study by Daniel Goldman, author of *Emotional Intelligence*, and *Social Intelligence*, that shows that "emotions spread from one person to another much like a cold, and that while it can be good to 'catch' an uplifting feeling, it can be damaging to take on others' feelings of anger, jealousy, anxiety, or hate."

So, if we want to feel good, it is extremely important to examine our relationships. Sometimes our best teachers are those with whom we have the most difficulty, and we can experience the most inner growth from interacting with those people. However, if we know that we can be positively or negatively affected by the relationships we have with others, we have to be very careful to limit the time we spend with toxic, chronically-negative people who always complain, who are always unhappy, who are always creating drama, and who are what I call "energy vampires." All of that drama can be extremely distracting, and is a waste of our time and energy. Stepping back from or letting go of a relationship that is unhealthy or toxic can be one of the healthiest moves to make. We can't change the people around us, but we *can* change the people we choose to be around.

It's up to each of us to heal ourselves. No one else can do it for us, and we cannot do it for someone else. We only have control over ourselves, and it's important for us not to create drama, too. Our job is to stay on our side of the street and do our own inner work. What someone else does is completely up to them. We can let them go while wishing them love and healing and, when we let those unhealthy relationships go, it creates a space, or opens a door for the Universe to bring an even better-suited person to us. As I went through this letting go process myself, I felt lonely at first, but once I had created that space, I found that I started meeting wonderful new people. I'm now blessed to have loving and healthy friendships with people I can truly trust, and I'm finally able to relax in the knowing that I no longer have to be on guard for any drama.

Meditation

"The best time to take a five-minute break to sit still, be quiet, and listen to your breathing is when you think you have the least time for it. The busier you are and the more overwhelmed you feel, the more you need the clarity and decluttering of meditation."

~ PH.D., GARY R. MCCLAIN

For those of you who don't meditate, you may be saying "oh my gosh, here we go again with that meditation message!" I can relate! I resisted, and resisted, and resisted meditating ... for years! My first experience with it was when I flew to Raleigh, North Carolina to attend Oprah's "Live Your Best Life" tour. Oprah and Cheryl Richardson spent the whole day sharing great insights into how to live a meaningful and enjoyable life. At one point Oprah encouraged those of us in the audience to close our eyes, take some deep breaths, silently ask "what am I here to learn?", and then be quiet for 15 minutes or so. There I sat, in perfect silence and as I found myself relaxing, I heard a voice say "To Love." It wasn't a real voice, it came from somewhere inside, and I remember feeling surprised and a little indignant at that answer. "To Love"???? I remember thinking, "I know how to love, what the heck are you talking about?" Immediately, I heard that voice again … and it said, "Yourself." Well, that shut me up. Bingo. It's exactly what I knew I still had to work on at that time of my life. I felt humbled and in awe of how powerful that answer was. I know that answer was the Truth with a capital "T."

That experience peaked my curiosity about meditation. I incorporated it more and more often, and even learned Transcendental Meditation, which is done twice a day for 20 minutes each time. I had never felt such a feeling of energized calm. I know that sounds contradictory, but I felt a deep calm inside, coupled with an increase in natural, calm energy. Meditation accomplishes two goals for me. It allows me to quiet both the inner and outer noise in my life. I credit meditation for my increased intuition, mental clarity, and for helping me feel the guidance from God, the angels, my guides, and my higher self.

Do I meditate twice a day, every day? No. When I do, however, I feel SO much better! I've learned not to beat myself up when I skip a few meditations. As a single mom of two busy teenagers, I do my best! Meditation for me is like a mini vacation, twice a day. It's an opportunity to listen to my soul and is a way to feel deep, inner peace. I would highly, highly recommend it. Even if all you can do is sit still, turn off the phone, close your eyes and breathe for five minutes, it will be beneficial. I promise!

Silence the external noise

❧ "If you listen closely enough to the silence, you may just hear something incredible: You."

~ JEFF FOSTER

Have you noticed that we seem to be moving at a faster pace than ever, and that we're exposed to more noise and information than ever? In Shawn Achor's book *before happiness: the 5 hidden keys to achieving success, spreading happiness, and sustaining positive changes* he cites a report that shows that per capita time spent consuming information in American households increased by 60% between 1980 and 2008. Wow! As humans, part of our natural instinct is to pay attention to sounds and stimuli around us—it's part of our survival instinct. Our minds are constantly trying to differentiate between important information and unimportant information. However, our brains can only pay attention to a certain amount of information at one time.

When we go on brain overload, it takes a toll on our health and well-being, and keeps us from leading our best lives. Shawn Achor also shares in *before happiness* that, according to research in positive psychology and neuroscience, by consciously decreasing the flood of information our brains receive by just 5 percent, we can improve our chances of boosting the positive signals that our brains receive which will point us to better decisions, improved health, and greater achievement.

So how can we do that? Since everyone is different, my suggestion is to pick a day, and set the intention to pay very close attention to how you feel throughout that day. Notice what sounds and stimuli are pleasant for you, and which ones bother you. It's what I did during that extremely stressful time in my life. I then made a plan. For me, it meant limiting my time watching television, muting the commercials when I did watch television, avoiding violent or noisy television shows, and discontinuing the habit of watching the same news stories over and over. I stopped obsessively checking my e-mail and limited it to only looking at it several times a day. I turned the ringer off on my phone when I needed to focus on a task. I avoided noisy places when I could, and would avoid busy traffic whenever possible. I made many more changes, and as I did, I began to feel much calmer. That, along with the inner work I was doing enabled me to feel better and better every day.

So although that period of time of overwhelm was very difficult me, the gift it provided was that it gave me the awareness that we all create our own reality through the Law of Attraction. The lessons I learned were that I needed to pay attention to my thoughts, practice self-love, eliminate drama and dysfunction in my life, and quiet my mind and outside noise so I could hear the beautiful messages my soul and God give me every day.

I'm so grateful that I can experience the richness that life has to offer, and to feel true happiness! As a life coach, I now delight in guiding others to experience their own healing so they, too, can be more aware and lead happier, more vibrant lives filled with kick-ass joy!

To all of my soul sisters on this life journey with me. Thank you for inspiring me to reach for my highest self by your example. I am in awe of you.

Dedicated to my daughters, Tatiana and Isabella. You are both so beautiful, inside and out. I am constantly amazed by your inner wisdom and ability to clearly see the truth. Thank you for blessing me with the honor of being your mother. May you always know your worth, have inner peace, and live the life of your dreams. I love you.

~Valentina Galante

Catherine Madeira

CATHERINE MADEIRA is a freelance writer and artist and has been receiving ethereal information for years and is now sharing it in the hope of helping others in their life's journeys. She is from the Reno / Tahoe area with her 2 children, Jason who has always demanded an intellectual approach to life, and Daughter, Kendal, who was born a very old soul. Catherine has a supportive, open-minded mother who allowed her eccentricities to expand. Subsequently, she has been able to receive, evaluate, and compile the information to pass to others.

Umbriel03@gmail.com

Memory From Another
Time and Place

It is of primary importance that whomever reads the following, does so with the understanding that it should be viewed not as a fantasy or fictional telling, but that I relay it to you with full belief in the truth of the occurrence and the truth of its purpose, necessity and value of the result. An additional reason to give serious thought to the reality of this memory. To understand that this series of events, their purpose, are a thing I had never before heard of, a process that I couldn't have possibly imagined but stemmed from total logic throughout.

The time frame of the memory is unknown to me, it was either countless ages ago or eons in the future. The location is also unknown to me other than, it was a lush clean wonderful place, my mind equated it to South America or it could have been an entirely different place, or planet.

The Dream opens. I am looking down at my bare feet, there's a band around my left ankle made of a white substance, possibly shells and a brown leather tie. I was wearing a short brown leather loincloth around my waist which was covering my genitals. At no time did I see a reflection of myself so I don't know what I looked like. I do know that I was a young man approximately 16 years old, as were the other young men I saw in this place.

The ground I was walking on was short green and grassy, alive with growth. The air was wonderfully warm not as humid as a rain forest but with similar components in the type of foliage of a rain forest. I was walking between two buildings made of light gray granite like stone. These structures were large. One structure was five feet to my right and the other was 12 feet to my left. I did not gaze up at them (I had been seeing them all my life) but my feeling is that they jutted off at a stair step angle, much like the pyramids here. I walked about 30 yards clearing the corners of the buildings. I came to a larger path, 30 feet across. Looking to my right I saw that I was near the edge of the village, the forest began just beyond the building to my right.

I then noticed what seemed to be the chief, or an elder. He had long black straight hair. On his head was a simple unadorned head dress, he had a dangling necklace that looked similar to the anklet I wore and brown leather loin cloth, bare feet and reddish colored cape, in his hand a tall wooden staff. I thought he looked wise and enviably noble. His face was unwrinkled, and seemed to be confident in every thought, move, word, or direction. I believe he was a man I would like to know and emulate. He did not command respect, he just had it. He appeared relaxed, while waiting for me and the six additional young men who would also participate, one of which was my best friend. His straight thick brown hair was neat and clean. My friend had a choker also of the white shells or beads. He had brown eyes. I knew we had experienced many boyhood adventures together and we knew each other well. When I saw the other young men I assumed I must look similar. We were small, five feet tall. The chief was taller 5/5 or 5/6. We were all lean and muscled. We were handsome with clear complexions, darkened skin, and white teeth. We could have been Mayan, but I am not sure. We were seemingly healthy and pleasant. Everyone was quiet at this moment but not intimidated or nervous about our meeting.

I don't know how large the village was but as I turned to walk towards the elder, behind me to my left was the rest of the village. The other granite buildings were far apart, in amongst trees and various foliage. I didn't see anyone else in the village.

It was early in the morning but the temperature was very pleasant. There were not clouds, no dew dripping off the leaves, the foliage was fairly thick. My feeling is that we were high in altitude because I didn't see any mountains.

My friend, the 5 others and I joined the elder. I don't remember any of us speaking. We formed a line, the elder turned and proceeded to follow a path into the forest. The plants varied widely. Some were much like ferns, others were plants I've never seen, with large green leaves. Occasionally on the side of the path there would be a granite-like boulder or rock. My instincts were that we walked in a southerly direction. We walked for a long time. Probably 3 or 4 hours. Other than the sounds of the birds in the trees, we encountered no other wildlife. Eventually we angled upward at a gentle slope.

As we reached the top of the hill, the living forest opened up into a clearing. In the clearing at the top of the hill was a building. The granite rectangular building was very plain with no decoration. Near the right end of the building there was an opening or doorway. It was squared off and the size of a normal door. The roof was flat. The sky above was indescribably clear blue.

We walked to the door. The elder stopped and stood to the left of the door. We all filed past him and into the building. Directly across from the door was a span to the opposing wall. In that wall was a highly set rectangular window, it appeared to be five feet long by three feet high. By the door and window I could tell that the walls were about eight inches thick. Through the window I could see some big leaves and the blue sky. The only light in the building was provided by this window and the entrance. The inside of the building was not like the outside. The inside floor, walls, and ceiling, were a dark red and dark grey swirling clay. The inside was damp with moisture as was the air, and was noticeably cooler than outside. The purpose for the offset door revealed itself after entering the structure. Directly in the center of the building was a wall. It separated the interior in half. The wall was made of the red and grey clay and was also very thick, "eight inches". It went from floor to ceiling and wall to wall cutting off access to the other side. In the wall there were Octagonal holes (same size and shape as our stop signs). They were seven evenly spaced openings across that center wall, they were three high from floor to ceiling, so 21 total openings in the wall. Through those cut outs I could see the other room on the other side of the structure. The seven Octagons across the center of the wall were (head high) and were all filled with the soft, red, grey, wet clay, packed tightly, filling in the entire eight inch thick space.

The elder followed us into the room, no one spoke. We instinctively knew what we had to do next. The nature of this ceremony did not require words between us, but silence was not ordered or requested in any way. We were not a people living under the hand of dominance of any individual or group. The quiet nature welled from profound respect for the purpose for the ceremony, and we were humbled in that we had been chosen to partake in this unknown ascension. The entire ceremony was quite uncomplicated in view of the extreme importance of its purpose.

We stood in line. The first young man facing the first clay filled hole in the wall. I was the last person in line. My best friend stood just in front of me. The first young man stepped to the clay filled Octagon. He raised his hands up next to his face, his fingers spread wide. He then gently pressed his hands and face into the clay filled space. The soft material accepted the imprint of his hands and face, as he stepped back from the wall the clay presented a perfect portrait of him. He took one side step and in a natural unison he stepped forward in time with the second participant. He embedded his form into the second mold as the number two man erased the reflection of his predecessor and replaced it with the imprint of his own hands and face. Again the two men stepped back and man number three added himself to the movement, in unison three men now stepped up. The first introducing his reflection to the third mold, man number two erasing the second imprint of man number one and man number three temporarily dominating the first hole with his figure. On it went one man adding himself to the smooth quiet movement, step forward, immersion, step back, and step side. Number five, on to number six and on to me, the seventh man.

My hands raised next to my face, fingers spread. Looking straight ahead, now we all step forward to meet the seven windows of vision. As I moved those final inches towards the replica of my dear friends facial imprint, I could smell the wet clay. I closed my eyes, the clay was pleasantly cool to my hands and face, I felt myself enveloped as I immersed my imprint over the reflection of my friends image. I found that I was not erasing the face of my friend, I was absorbing it. I would have been stunned and confused by the instantaneous effects of what followed, but with the unexpected walked the all-knowing.

I came to this place barring the knowledge of only my life's experience. At the instant I touched the clay I first realized that I held the memory of (me) looking at me from a different place. It took only a millisecond to understand that I was seeing me through my friends' eyes. Recalling a memory we both had, as at that time we were together. But seeing it now from two perspectives. Now all at once I realized that in every aspect conceivable I had inherited not only his memories, thoughts and feelings, but also of the others. More over the joining with the clay bestowed to me the entire memory, knowledge and life experience of all who preceded me to this place and did this thing (sharing their souls) back to our peoples beginning.

I should have fallen, stunned to a catatonic state at the onset of the enormous, instant, inundation of information into my being, but just the opposite was the case. Along with the collision of awareness came the understanding of its origin, purpose and necessity. Vaulting from age 16 to an age unknown, and able to receive and utilize the information just as those who experienced and shared before me. Three seconds ago this was new and mysterious, three seconds hence I had undertaken the absorption countless times. Suddenly the noble mysterious elder was an old friend. One who I took the ritual with when he was a young man so many years ago.

In unison with my companions I pulled my head and hands from the clay, stepped back, stepped side, I imprinted myself in the second space in time with the other participants. This continued on until I, being last had imprinted myself in the last clay mold. As soon as I stepped away from the wall the clay filled openings began to gently break apart and fall into the opposing room, leaving only the open Octagon windows.

The ceremony complete, we silently exited the place of memories. Unaffected emotionally as we were all now ancient and had done this so many times before.

As we began our walk home (my) dream began to fade and ended. The information I needed to absorb was complete. I am honored to have been shown this passage, its purpose, system and success through the ages.

The humble nature of the chosen young me and the privilege of receiving such a gift and responsibility was a thing generally unspoken. We were chosen without notice of others. Our new knowledge was not necessarily shared with the masses. This passing of memory was done to keep alive the history of our civilization. Obviously the boys returned as men (ancient men). But with the expansion also came the ability to calm the overwhelming nature and output of the wisdom. Moving and living amongst their people with the existence of what they held, basically unknown to the others. If things needed assistance the men could draw on their ancient wisdom to help the community through whatever problems arose. It was their job to take care of their people. They were looked upon as quiet elders, but tried not to draw attention to themselves. It was not secrecy with control or malice at its base. It was a simple way to ensure the history remain exactly intact.

Our understanding was, that of the original seven men, the last living man in the proceeding group made sure the next generation was chosen and taken to the place for the passing of memory to help secure their continued civilizations legacy.

The astonishing impact involved in this quiet process was born of logic and their knowledge that souls carry their entire history intact and available for any of us to draw from. I'm not sure how it worked. I currently don't know the significance of the seven windows. Maybe it took seven to complete the upload of information. Also in the room there was a total of 21 windows, 14 of which were not used. I think we immersed our hands and face because our hands transfer so much energy. Our hands heal and create, we project power from our hands. Was it the place, some mystical component in the clay? Joining the clay and each other, coupled with the belief that such a thing is possible. This triad enabling them to touch their point of origin.

I wonder, if this was a memory of the future, when I do submerge my hands and face into the clay, if the distant recollection of me, now, in this life will present itself, and be added to the memory line. Will I live again in the mind of the young man I am in the future? On the reverse side, I was shown the memory of this past or future life and experience. So the young stranger lives with me now and has been added to my line. Either way, past or future, I remember, the experience is mine, and I have been infused with the responsibility to share it with you.

In a similar way we, here, in this place, are also able to draw upon eternity. It's ours, our memory (past or future) to see and use if we choose to. It's as simple as opening yourself to the tidal wave of understanding. Believe what comes to you. The more you believe the more you will be given.

Dedicated to my Granddaughter, Harlo Monroe, who reintroduced me to the gravity of life. To my two tiny dogs—Bell, my best friend and angel on Earth, and Bee, Bell's lively assistant. My Father, Richard, who passed years ago but has stayed to watch over me.

Lisa Hardwick-Peplow and Nancy Newman, of Visionary Insight Press, for giving me the opportunity to share my information. Without these two wonderful, accepting people I may have lived my life without being able to complete my purpose for coming here. To my dear friend, Shari Pannell, who introduced me to the Nancy and Lisa of Visionary Insight Press. Also, to my sister, Rochelle, and her daughter, Robin Rash, (a budding author) who helped me clean up my story. Finally to Chelle Thompson, Visionary Insight Press' Editor-At-Large, for proof reading my work.

~Catherine Madeira

From the stars

"she came from the stars. it was
her job to remember that, to
hold that, and to honor that."

~ TERRI ST. CLOUD
www.BoneSighArts.com

Mickey Mackaben

MICKEY MACKABEN is a first time author, professional hairdresser with 29 years of experience, entrepreneur, mentor, and Reiki Level III Practitioner. For 13 years she was an International Educator, Platform Artist, Color Educator and "Train the Trainer" educator with Paul Mitchell. She has been published twice in Modern Salon and created images for national ad campaigns while working at JCPenney Salon.

She has been in tune with her authentic self since before she knew what that meant. Drawing from her own experiences and the many teachers around her, she teaches others and helps them cultivate their authentic self.

www.facebook.com/salontransitionsbymickey

 Intention

When I was asked to contribute to this wonderful project, I was laid up in incredible pain wondering if maybe I should have chosen to go the doctor's office for my pain medication, not the aisles of Walgreens. As I finished reading Lisa's email asking me to do this, my first thoughts were full of doubt.

I thought to myself, "I'm not an author, I don't know how to do this. Oh my gosh, this scares me!" But soon my thought changed to, "Yep, you're gonna do this and you can."

I decided I better reply quickly before I changed my mind. I began, "Lisa, I would love to share my awakening journey that never ends. My *intention* … " and in that moment I didn't know what I would write about. I didn't know what my *intention* was going to be. So I decided to put my phone down, take a little nap, and come back to it.

When I awoke from my nap, I opened my email to finish my draft and saw that Lisa had responded to me, "I'm thrilled you are going to be part of this project, writing about *intention*. Woooohooo!" I paused, a little perplexed. "Okay, I guess I'm going to write about *intention*."

I was really confused though; I didn't know what had happened. Well, somehow my phone magically sent that email off before it was complete, at least in the way I thought it should be.

You see … we are so powerful beyond what we even realize, that I had mindlessly already sent out to the universe my *intention*. At that moment, my intention was formed as a question in my mind … "What will I write about?" Before I had a chance to even realize this was my **intention**, I already had begun to draw it to me. That is how I came to write about **intention**.

Funny thing about intention is that it shows up in ways you may not recognize were even intentions. I believe this happens because we set intentions on more than one level. What I have found to be true for me is that I set my intentions on three levels: mind, heart, and soul.

Mind ... thoughts
Heart ... feelings, emotions
Soul ... the "I am"—the knowing, the blueprint

When you state your intention, you begin to draw to you that which you need to support what is being physically created. What you intend is what you're creating.

It begins in your mind

Mindful or mindless, my thoughts contribute to my intention. Knowing why I am choosing to do something and why I want something helps me identify my intention and be mindful of what I am creating.

Have you ever had a time in life that you created your intention in a way you did not intend? I certainly have. Then life smacked me in the face and said, "Wake up girl ... WAKE UP GIRL!"

About three years ago, I found myself in a position I never thought could happen to me. I was worried I would lose my house. My business had slowed. I had ended a two-year relationship that I though would result in a marriage or long term commitment. I had started menopause, well pre-menopause.

Okay ... so we all know, or some of us know pre-menopause can kick your booty. And boy, it truly does! Your emotions are like you're frickin' fourteen again. **OH. MY. GOD.** I don't know who would EVER want to be that age again. It's terrible! You're up. You're down. You're sideways. You don't even know what you're thinking. Your body is changing, just like when you were a teenager. You go through it all again, just on the other side of it, it's not as pleasant. So, take all of these things happening, throw in a twisted version of puberty and I was a complete wreck.

I was so exhausted and tired by life. I was pressed. I just really needed a time out ... but I couldn't give it to myself.

By not stopping and taking that time out I so needed, I created all this craziness in my life. It was so stressful and so frustrating. I'm pretty sure I gained twenty pounds in the process and chased everybody away who cared about me because I was not fun to be around. I was so low; I really didn't think I could get any lower. I felt like that person in everyone's life that is supposed to be the pillar; and the pillar is crumbling and breaking, but because the pillar is so stoic nothing can penetrate and no one can see. I didn't want anyone to know because I was afraid. I was afraid that everything I had worked so hard for could be gone in a moment. I was afraid that somehow I had failed. What might people think? WHAT might people think? I'm not strong? I'm not worthy? I'm not capable?

I FINALLY just had to share with my son and his wife what was going on. I couldn't take it anymore; I just had to tell someone. And so, I did. And it was hard. It was really hard. The hardest part was realizing that I had created it.

The good news is that I did find my way. I realized, during the process, that what I wanted all along was a time out, I just needed a moment to pause my life and reflect and reset. Out of not honoring that, my mind worked alone in creating this intention. It showed up in what could have been a devastating outcome. This is why it is important to bring your intention from your mind down to your heart, before it physically manifests.

Bring it down to your heart

I bring it down to my heart by finding a comfortable, quiet place to sit. Maybe it's a chair, couch, or maybe it'll be in my bed. Just somewhere that feels peaceful to me in that moment. I close my eyes and allow my thoughts to flow. Most of my initial thoughts are just chitchat, my mind clearing and letting go. As my thoughts keep flowing, the truth of what I'm feeling becomes clearer. I begin deciding which thoughts to keep and which to release. I believe … they call this meditation (teehee). If I decide to "keep" a thought, I write it down in my journal or sometimes I just pick up a notebook that's handy and start to write.

After I write each thought I go back and ask myself how I *feel* about it. If I have a strong feeling (or reaction), good or bad, then I continue with it to the next level. Some thoughts you are meant to feel, then release, not physically manifest. You will know which ones those are, trust yourself on this process … your soul will guide you. You know, that feeling in your stomach? No need to over think it.

Once I've gotten it down to my current intention that I want to physically manifest, I like to do something visual.

"COLLAGES!" (Insert singing voice)

I make collages, all types. Sometimes I make large ones (I love giant poster board) that include every intention, or sometimes I make smaller, more specific ones that I then group together … because really, I like large ones. I draw pictures, I cut out words and images, and I bust out the glitter glue. I just make it fun and engage my emotions and feelings. I use these images to help me tune in to what my intention will *feel* like. After I prettify it, I hang it up where I see it … all … the … time.

The universe only knows the thoughts you think are real, so by seeing and feeling your intentions you are already drawing them to you. Be patient. Keep connecting to how your **intention** will feel when physically manifested.

You will get there regardless

Your soul is your blueprint, and your blueprint doesn't change. Your soul is always driving you. It is always talking to and communicating with you. Sometimes the communication is subtle, sometimes not so subtle, kind of like my earlier story where the universe and my soul were calling me to wake up. This is why it is important to engage your mind and your heart, to connect to and hear the soul.

"You are always going to get where you are meant to be," Soul says, "you decide how hard or easy the journey will be."

I dedicate this writing to three of my greatest teachers, my children Britny Danielle, Kirk Idrees, and Tempest Dayne.

Thank you for your unconditional love. Always my love is with you!

Thank you Britny Danielle for helping me edit my message, putting words to paper is much different than sharing thoughts verbally. You always amaze me.

Gratitude to all my friends and family for seeing in me things I can't always see in myself. Much love to you all!

~Mickey Mackaben

Make it

"to have joy you must make it.
and take it. saying you want
it isn't enough. maybe that's
with everything ... saying you
want it isn't enough. make it.
take it. know it's yours."

~ TERRI ST. CLOUD
www.BoneSighArts.com

Cindy Ray

CINDY RAY is a Certified Life Coach, Author, and Workshop Facilitator with over fifteen years experience. She specializes in Personal Growth, Relationship, and Parenting Education. Cindy also writes children's books and fiction novels.

www.facebook.com/Cindy.Ray.Author

A Peace of Cake

"I suffer because my interactions with others do
not meet the expectations I did not know I had."

~ JIM MCDONALD

Everyone kept telling me I needed to let him go, but no one told me how. Then one day, I answered the phone, but it wasn't him on the other end. The call was coming from his cell phone, but as soon as I heard a woman's voice, I immediately knew what the deal was. She didn't need to explain that she was also his fiancé, or that she would fight for him. She didn't need to call me names or threaten me. I told her there would be no fight, she could have him. It only took a few seconds for me to let him go.

As I hung up the phone in disbelief, I noticed something unusual. I was extremely calm. I didn't cry, I didn't scream, I just sat there, thinking about the phone call, and how I didn't even ask her name. An hour later, when my roommate came home, I told him what happened. He asked me how I could be so calm after learning I'd been dating a cheater. In fact, I had moved across the country to be with him. I didn't know why I was so calm, but the answer would come to me later.

I expected a flood of tears and drama. I had been cheated on before, and I had never reacted this way. It was as if I were observing the whole thing from outside of myself. I was trying to sort out what had just happened. He was out of town, he said, on a business trip when I received the call. As I replayed the moments of the previous weeks, I recall feeling like he was hiding something. There were moments when he was loving and reassuring, but I suspected he wasn't being honest about the trip. He called me from the plane, and told me how much he loved me. I didn't push for details when he insisted to me that it was just business. I probably didn't want to know the truth.

Now, I began to get really curious about the whole thing, about our relationship, and why we kept breaking up again and again. He was free to decide who he wanted to be with, and he had already made the plans to go out of town before we reconciled this last time. He could have easily gone on with this other relationship if he wanted someone else. It felt as though he was deliberately trying to hurt me. I knew I had to keep looking for the reason this all happened. If I just walked away without looking, I would always feel like his victim. I would carry that energy into any future relationships, and the pattern would repeat itself.

Fact is, he was a selfish jerk, with no morals or character. When I talked to my Lifecoach, he told me that I was taking the high road, trying to take responsibility for the failure of the relationship. I was making excuses for the creep who had cheated on me after everything I had done for him. Although I knew I had to take responsibility for creating my life, I didn't have to take on the mess that *he* brought into it. His cheating was about his character, not my inadequacies. And I wanted closure, even though I didn't know what it would look like. I wanted to know *why*. I sent him a few emails the next day, demanding an explanation. I never got one. He was probably suspicious that I might be plotting his murder. I knew I would have to close that chapter in my own way. Maybe closure is our way of staying connected for a little while longer, to ease out of the pain. Can anything they say actually make us feel better? "It's not you, it's me." Well, that always made it worse! Seeking closure seems to have the opposite effect. It keeps you focused on the failed relationship instead of moving on, or looking to see how you really didn't want the relationship anyway, but you were too powerless or afraid to end it yourself.

Seeking closure is the same thing as trying to get your self-love from outside of you. It can't be done. The answer for why it ended is *always* inside of you. You have to get curious enough and willing enough to look beyond the appearance of things to see it. Yes, I said that you didn't want the relationship, just like I didn't want the relationship with the cheater. My ego wanted to hang on. I thought if I loved him enough, he would change. I also thought that he was broken and I could fix him. Boy, was my ego large!

I began to look, really pay attention. I rewound the tape in my mind to the exact moment when I decided he wasn't for me. (There were a number of things that I won't go into, but deal breakers for me.) I also tried to rewrite the tape to produce a different outcome. I couldn't do it. Once I decided that he wasn't right for me, I energetically sent out a vibe telling him my thoughts, and he began the process of dumping me. If only I'd had the guts to do the dirty work myself.

So, if you are paying close attention, you will see that when someone dumps you, you wanted them to. You lacked the courage to end it. No one wants to be the bad guy. The bad guy doesn't get to eat ice cream, go on endless chocolate binges and whine to their friends about the injustice of it all. The bad guy just moves on. They move on to the next thing they want, while the victim stays stuck, looking for closure, and blaming the bad guy. We can take a lesson from the bad guy. Move on to the next thing that you want, instead of staying stuck.

That strange calmness I was feeling when I found out he had been cheating on me was actually relief. I know this now, because I have never regretted losing him. He has contacted me since, wanting my forgiveness and friendship. I have no desire to rekindle any sort of relationship with him, and I have never felt more free.

We are all made up of energy. We all emit a vibrational frequency similar to radio waves. The people in our lives respond to the vibes we are putting out. If you don't believe me, then try this: when you are having a conversation with someone, anyone, deliberately change your thoughts so that they don't match your words. For example, if you are talking with your friend, tell them how much you like the shirt they are wearing while thinking that it's the most hideous and disgusting thing you've ever seen. If you want to go further, think of a few unkind things about your friend too. Try to sound believable while holding a different thought.

Then afterward, ask them if they could tell you were thinking something different. You may be surprised by what they tell you. Then go ahead and think of some really good things about your friend. You'll want to shift the negative energy. If they get upset with you, then share with them what you were doing. After you do this a few times, you will get it about the vibe you are putting out. It's not the words, it's the intention behind them. Maintaining your vibrational energy is very important.

Once you stop feeling like a victim, you will begin to see that you are creating your life and your relationships. Once you really, really get this, then you can start deliberately creating what you want.

Most people think that life happens to them. 99% of the world's population operates from the "victim" mentality. If you want to join the 1% to operate from a "manifesting" mentality, then you have to understand that you are in control. You are the author of the screenplay of your life. You hand out the scripts to your family, friends, and any person that's in your awareness. If you don't like what they are saying and doing, hand them a new script. How do you do that? You look inward. You decide what you want your relationships to look like, to feel like, to be.

All of the people in your life are merely a reflection of how you see yourself. Have you ever noticed that your friends, and especially your family, seem to bring out your biggest insecurities that you have about yourself? When you focus on what you adore and love about you, those things are also reflected. People treat you the same way you treat yourself. I know you've heard this before, but how do you put it into practice? For real, to change your life? To have that peace of mind? Keep reading.

Since we are on the subject of relationships, I'll begin with those steps. Even if you are the one to end things, there needs to be a grieving process for what you've given up. Begin by crying that shit out, as loud and as long as you need to. Make a ritual out of it. Get your stash of comfort items, whether it be a bottle of wine, chocolate, or a gallon of ice cream. Make a playlist of the saddest songs you know. You want to really feel the loss and sadness. Design the grieving process how you need it to go. And hang in there, it gets better!

When that part is over, begin the process of thinking about it, logically. Usually when we are emotionally attached to someone, logic goes out the window. Bring it back in. Rewind those tapes and see where you pushed them away, and when you gave up. This always makes me feel better, to know I was the one who chose how it went. One day you may feel like you got this and think the pain is behind you. Then the very next day feel like a basket case and like you haven't progressed at all. Two steps forward and one step back. Keep going. It's natural to go through the whole range of emotions.

It's funny how we think we need someone, or think we can't live without them. Then a day passes and they're not in it, and you survive. Then another day passes and one day you realize you put them on a pedestal and gave them more importance than they deserved. Nothing feels as good as letting go.

I highly recommend listening to guided meditations, not in place of therapy, but in addition to what you are already doing. YouTube has millions of videos you can listen to with headphones. I have several playlists that consist of everything from manifesting money to improving my memory. My favorites are the Theta Beats. They also help me to fall asleep, especially if I am anxious or worried. Meditation is my number one tool for being in a peaceful state of mind.

Next, stop giving your power to other people and entities. There's no higher plan for you than the one you have for yourself. Too many times we say it's not God's plan or destiny or whatever. How about if you get to make your own plan? You get to decide who you let in, who you love, who you spend time with, how much money you make, what job you have, and so on. The possibilities are endless.

If you don't like where you are, change it in your mind first. You hate your job, but can't quit just yet, decide what you want to do. How much money do you want to make? You are single and can't seem to find a mate? Decide what type of person you want to be with, and what characteristics they have. Where do you want to live? What does your house look like?

Write out your goals, in detail. If you write it into a story, with lots of feeling words, it helps manifest it quicker. Imagine waking up and being grateful for everything in your life. You have the perfect partner, you drive your dream car to your ideal job, where you make more than enough money to buy anything you want. You vacation in beautiful, exotic locations, with your love by your side. You have a loving family, and live the good life. These are some examples, you get to write your story.

After you have your story just the way you want it, the most important thing you can do with it, is to read it. Read it every single morning and every night before you go to sleep. Don't just go through the motions, read it with all of the emotion of feeling like it's real. Focus on that diligently for a few weeks or months. You don't know it yet, but you get to decide how long it takes for things to change.

Taking responsibility for your frame of mind is a good way to head off other people ruining your day. It's impossible to avoid negative or inconsiderate people, but it's easier to deal with them when you are already in a good mood. And the more you practice being in control of your feelings, the less you are affected by other people's negativity.

I also have a gratitude list that I read many times a day. In fact, I have it memorized and I say it every time I get into my car, sort of a habit. I speak it in the present tense, and it's a prayer for what I want. Being grateful is an excellent way to attract the things and events that I desire.

The next part may be the hardest of all. You must stop complaining. You can't be rich or have peace of mind if you are complaining all the time. If you count how many times in one hour you complain or have negative thoughts, it would probably amount to hundreds. Don't post your bad luck on social media, it multiplies every time someone reads it. If you must rant, do so and then remove it within a short period of time. Then post something positive to shift the energy.

I had a hard time with not feeling like a victim after my divorce. I felt thrown away and left out in the cold. It took a lot of work for me to realize he didn't do anything to me and that I was in complete control of everything that I felt, and that I even had a part in the creation of the events. The financial hardships that I experienced were the evidence of my thoughts. I kept looking back and dwelling on what I had lost and what I had given up. Those thoughts were keeping me broke. I had to constantly remind myself that he was not the source of my income or anything that I had. When I began to shift into manifesting mentality, the money started showing up.

My path to peace began over a decade ago when I participated in a weekend workshop that focused on letting go of blame. I began with the attitude that I had every right to blame my parents, my spouse, my kids, or anyone else I felt had wronged me. By the end of the weekend, after I forgave the one person for whom I held the most contempt, I was in a state of complete bliss. It literally felt as though the world had been lifted off of my shoulders. I half expected it to wear off the next day, but it lasted for over three months. I think it ended because I thought it would. When I recall how peaceful I felt letting go of the blame, it reminds me that my emotions and feelings are my choice. *I get to decide my level of serenity in any situation.*

It seems that when I begin a project like this, writing about how to remain peaceful, all kinds of chaos breaks out in my life. It's really challenging to be peaceful when I'm murdering everyone in my head. Things that would ordinarily not bother me seem to get on my last nerve. Even the builder quit working on my new house, leaving me to wonder if I will ever get to move into my dream home.

So, in this moment, I am reminded that empathy, compassion, and forgiveness are the keys to my peace of mind. I have no idea what struggles my builder is having, or if some tragedy has befallen him. I've been dwelling on how the delays are affecting me, putting me out. Instead, I will focus on sending him loving and positive thoughts. I don't know if it will change anything, but I sure feel better and more at peace.

Forrest Gump said life is like a box of chocolates, you never know what you're going to get. I think it's more like a piece of cake, and I get to choose EXACTLY what I'm going to get.

Dedicated to my daughters, Rebecca and Reagan Chauff, and my grandson, Nathan Newell. You guys are the best family, and dearest friends. I love you all, you are the best part of my life.

To my devoted fans and friends, I am forever grateful for your support. I am blessed to have a huge list of people who inspire and help me every day, and you all mean so much to me. Special thanks to Matt Crawford, who makes my hair beautiful.

~Cindy Ray

Tina Gibson

TINA GIBSON is an international speaker, author and teacher in the area of self discovery. She is also a life-coach and Spiritual Practitioner assisting others to better understand their personal power. Having traveled extensively around the globe, Tina inspires many to live in and come from a place of love. After spending years learning the true power of self-love, she shares her journey and the challenges she has experienced by her own limiting beliefs. The mother of 3 successful sons, Tina continues to share her message of the gifts of self-love. Tina resides in Albuquerque, New Mexico.

tina@thesoulsway.com
www.thesoulsway.com

 The Dungeon

Musty and stale, the darkness below hits me, the damp air sudden. Opening the dungeon door, the old wooden steps show me the way. I must go down there, and yet the thought of what lies beneath sends electric chills down my back. Slowly though, I take the first step. The wood creaks and sways just a little. Gathering composure, I continue to the second. Another creak and an eerie moan of rotting wood speaks to me, telling me the time, reminding me of the years that have passed. Descending into the chamber, I feel the room. It reeks of dread. A cold draft pricks my skin just as my eyes begin to adjust to the absence of light. I can feel the suffering.

Moving in closer, I see cobblestone walls and chains hanging in the cell. It seems empty, but I know she is there. Perhaps, the shadows know where she sleeps. A slight movement in the corner holds me, and paralyzed, I stand there unable to move.

Instantly, two eyes open. The whites shining like candles, light the cell and the person who is there. Her hair, matted against a face smeared with filth, hangs in strings around her slight frame. Her hollow eyes with dark circles speak only of the time she has spent in this dreary hole, locked away from the world above.

At first, only a whimper escapes her. Then she jumps up. The chains holding her clang to the stone floor as she moves. Grasping the iron bars, she sobs. Her wails echo through the darkness and into my heart, penetrating me like arrows piercing the flesh of a hunted gazelle.

Overwhelmed by sadness, the ache in my gut goes deep; my stomach lurches as I watch her pleading face. Somehow, I didn't expect this. I know her, it's true, but I didn't think I would find her this frail. I did not think she would be this small. She is only a child. She can't be more than seven.

Now, aware of the need to find the key, I search frantically. It has to be here. Watching closely, instantly and with sudden anger she cries out, "Why can't you find the key?" I hear her mucous filled voice for the first time. In desperation, she shouts again, "I hate you! Why won't you get me out of here?" Flailing her body with no attempt to control her temper, she throws herself into a fit of rage.

My first thoughts are filled with contempt. Why is she acting like this? No wonder she has been locked away for so long. What a brat. Why did I return here? Furious thoughts begin to run wild, but instead, I take a deep breath. I can do it differently this time. Quietly, I remember, and with another breath, I consider the reason I have returned.

It was about fifty years ago, so the exact time escapes me. I didn't like her then, but I want to like her now. I know why she acts this way. She has every reason to be angry. I have finally come to release her and take her out of this prison. I am the only one who can. No wonder she is angry and sad. I have come to realize, it all stems from me.

I look again at this beast of a child, her eyes on me like a panther stalking its prey. She roams the cell, pacing. I know she wants freedom. I feel her soul reaching out, reaching to me, and beckoning me closer. She knows me from the past. It is true.

Like her, I was just a child. We both enjoyed life and were curious, asking questions and observing the world around us. We liked to play and run, laugh and sing. But now—look at her! Ragged and sad, her smile is withered, her inquisitive personality gone. Her prison sentence has been so harsh. She does not play; she does not sing. She is not happy. I know ... I know because she *is* me.

She is me when I was young. She lived in a world of right and wrong, good and bad, of judgments and people-pleasing. I can still hear the grownups. They made statements in their adult kind of way, talking and analyzing, hurrying around and getting things done. I know what it is like to be an adult now. I understand their intentions, but she was too young! She sensitively listened to what other people said, and she took it in like a sponge soaking up spilled milk. She interpreted their words incorrectly and made herself wrong based on what they said, most of which was not even directed towards her. Many comments and actions of others left her believing the worst about herself. She felt inadequate. She didn't think she could measure up to their expectations. She didn't feel she was good enough. She felt there must be something wrong with her.

Continuing to believe herself bad and unworthy, she did something drastic. (I mean, *I* did something drastic.) I sabotaged myself and disassociated from my innocence. I did not want anybody to see my mistakes and insecurities. In my shame, I locked up my heart and turned away from myself—my little girl. I forced my naughty little self into a metaphorical deep, dark, dungeon, never to be seen again.

My inner child had remained in this dungeon, while the rest of me grew up. Out of self preservation, I lived in a state of temporary amnesia, forgetting what I did to her. The memory of her faded as I grew older. In time, I married and raised children. I educated myself and pursued a career. I lived my life hustling through it, meeting deadlines and taking care of the needs of others. I stood on the sidelines and cheered from the bleachers at my children's accomplishments. I kept a clean house. I was organized and seemingly able to multitask my life away. I had it all together—at least that's what it looked like on the outside. Yet inwardly, I was facing a world of hurt.

As I grew older, unhappiness and depressions plagued me and rose up like a well of contamination. Covering up my discontent became difficult. The façade wore thin my ability to compensate. I was waking up. Perhaps, this is what happens to people when they get older. A new kind of wisdom takes over. As I became more aware, I began to remember who I was. I remembered that little girl. I could hear her cries. I remembered her dreams and desires, and I caught glimpses of her anger.

Oh yes, I felt her anger. I felt that pointed surge of horrific agitation rising up, often for reasons that didn't make sense. Expressing my anger would not be tolerated. I knew I needed to stay in control. I needed to put a tight lid on my unexpressed feelings. On those occasions when anger got the best of me, guilt became my new best friend. It was a cycle of controlling the dragon inside, resenting its existence, and guilting myself for allowing its fiery voice to be heard.

A dragon. I had become the harborer of a creature that even frightened me. Why? I didn't understand where it came from and why I was so upset. My life was good. I had a loving family. My parents raised me to believe in God. I was an active child, and I had many friends. I enjoyed sports and music, took gymnastics lessons, swam on a swim team, and learned to play the violin. I was provided with the comforts of a middle class family in the 60s and 70s. So why was I angry? What was wrong with me?

Now as an adult, I know there wasn't anything wrong with me. I was pretty. I had dreams of a bright future. I was smart and a good student, memorizing the multiplication tables and history facts. Easily, I made friends. But somehow I felt I was not as good as the rest. I wonder why I didn't embrace who I was, and I have to wonder why I haven't fully embraced myself, even now.

More memories flood my thoughts. They take me into the past of my young motherhood. Ugh, I had no business being a mother at twenty-two. I didn't know what I was doing. I wish I had been a better mother. I could have spent more time with my children. I wish I had been more tolerant. Could I have enjoyed my sons more when they were young? Was I truly doing the best I could? How could anything have been more important than them? I wish I hadn't made those mistakes.

Still in the dungeon, remorseful thoughts come. Hell, I have made a lot of mistakes. Fiery pains of failed marriages scorch my heart. Flames of financial struggles suffocate me. Longings for joy rather than sadness overtake me and send me into the plagues of unspoken inner turmoil. "Oh," I utter between sobs, "I want a do-over! I want to do it again, but this time, I want to get it right! Please, I just want to make it right."

My mind struggles. Wondering and pondering, I consider my future and ask how my life can change if I don't do something different now. How can I reconcile the past? How can I let myself be free of guilt? I recognize my fate. A "do-over" would be nice, but that isn't going to happen. How can I be happy now?

My heartbeat quickens. Do I even like myself? I am aware I have allowed others to see only parts of me, and I consider the reasons I haven't shown myself completely. Why have I been afraid to voice my opinions? Do I really dislike myself that much?

Closing my eyes at the pain of these new thoughts, awareness overrides my sanity, and I rattle off some of the fears of my past: Not wanting to experience the embarrassment of being wrong, fear of ridicule and judgment, being unfairly accused, rejection, betrayal. Comments have hurt me, feelings of shame, disconnection and not belonging, even the fear of being alone.

In the dark my voice rings clear. This time with a fervent sounding, "What in the hell is so wrong with me that I would choose to keep myself hidden? Why have I chosen to escape my fear by turning my back on a preciousness that is in me?"

The girl, now in the corner, stirs. The sound of my voice still vibrates through the room's silence, but I continue, drowned in my thoughts. I realize her fate has always been at the root of my anger. Even when I rebelled and acted out, it was the feeling of neglect I acted upon. When

I reacted to situations, it was her pain and insecurity I was feeling. She, the little girl in me, felt afraid and scared, untrusting and saddened at being found guilty of inadequacy. She had wanted approval. She had wanted to be accepted and loved, and like a puppet, I acted out her deepest hurts. I had refused to see her as good. My heart was closed to her. I did not love her. In truth, I did not love myself.

Once again she moves in the shadows. She is like an abandoned kitten huddling in an alley, feral and mistrusting of the world. I know only warm milk and soothing tones would persuade a lost kitten from its hiding place, but what about her? What about me? What would coax me out of the darkness? There is only one thing.

I watch her staring at me, mistrusting my intentions. I want to save her. I want to save us both, but how do I prove to her I really care? How do I let her know I am not upset with her anymore and that everything about her is accepted by me now?

Sitting on that cold floor, I feel into my own heart and remember the child before me. My heart opens to her. My voice barely audible I whisper, "I want you back."

The look in her eyes is sudden. Enraged, she screams words I do not want to hear, "I hate you!"

A jolt of fury strikes me like a bolt of lightning, yet it dissipates into soft rain. Not wanting to react to harsh words, deeply hearing them instead, I put myself in her shoes and feel her despair. I want to hear her cries. Whispering again, my heart feels the lonely creature before me. "I love you."

"Don't say that!" Her words are clipped and short and filled with poison.

"Please come back to me. I am sorry," I answer. "I want you. I want you back."

"You did this to me." Her accusing tone pierces me, but again the words come gently, "Please come to me. I love you."

I feel her energy shift slightly; in the darkness, she moves and timidly stands.

"Come on," I whisper, reaching for her through the bars of her cell.

Gingerly, another step closer; she hesitates slightly. I encourage her again. Her hand is just out of my reach. Only the bars of the cell separate the woman I have become from the girl I discarded so long ago. Her eyes, unsure, focus on my outstretched hand. I plead for her to step closer. I know she just wants my acceptance.

"I am sorry, I am so sorry," I continue. The pain in my chest opens me even more. Weeping through fallen tears, I sob into the empty space between us. "I love you," and holding myself, the words come again. "I love you."

The real life episode that transpired before I walked into my imagined dungeon will be forever imprinted in my mind. Perhaps I will expand upon it in another venue someday, but I can say it was difficult and emotionally stirring; yet, I am grateful for it because I was broken open that day.

A family situation was taking place. I was upset and considered not speaking up at all. It was a pattern I had fallen into from childhood, but this time was different. Instead, of stifling the emotions, I let them out, and I chose to speak. The voice which had remained hidden for so long, tried her best to sound like an adult, but it was still the voice of a child, an angry little girl who hadn't yet learned to express herself very well. The voice of my child had been shut down for so long, even I couldn't make her sound better. I needed her to speak up that day. And she did.

Afterwards, I retreated to the bathroom and into a hot shower. My tears ran endlessly, and I collapsed onto the shower floor. Yet, while the water cascaded around me, the tears of my 50-year-old self and those of my abandoned child were one and the same. I coddled and loved that little girl in me, just like I would if my granddaughter were in pain. She held on to me like a baby needing her mother. I rocked her back and forth as my thoughts in the dungeon wildly took over, all while the shower ran.

In the dungeon I held her and spoke again, "I love you. I want you back." Like fairy dust magic and the speed of a flying carpet, the cell walls of the dungeon vaporized into sunlight. Bright and clean, that horrible, dark cell disappeared into the illusion from which it was created. The transformative moment left me and the little girl face-to-face, exposed and transparent, embraced by the elixir of my own heart. I felt love for her, but there was more. As my heart opened to her, she let go of her need to blame me. I felt forgiveness from her, and I realized I was forgiving myself.

Like a caterpillar emerging from its cocoon, we completed the metamorphosis. She took her rightful place in the safety of my heart, and I became whole. We were one again. The little girl and the adult, integrated, loved, and accepted.

It's interesting how self-acceptance relieves pain and anguish. Free of my own judgment, life's energy flowed in constant waves of softness, free to move through me without resistance. My blockages melted into nothingness.

I believe, accepting me and loving myself are one and the same. With full acceptance, there is no need to hide my human frailties or my mistakes and challenges because insecurity dwindles with acceptance, leaving the feeling of wellbeing instead. Now, I acknowledge my mistakes and challenges. They have served me in the past. They have helped me become the person I am today, and I have learned much from them. Yet, while I no longer need them, I choose to love them, too.

I am a powerful creative Being, a spiritual Being having a human experience. Yet, in that statement, I do not want to negate my humanness. I believe I have idealized my spirituality and minimized the human side of me. In doing so, I have made myself wrong for experiencing the discomforts and challenges I bring to my life. Accepting myself means I activate my heart and send love to all of me, not just the areas I like.

An energy shift takes place as I embrace myself fully. My heart energy eliminates the need to guard myself from hurts and judgments, judgments which actually came from me, not from them. Without love, there is resistance. In the face of resistance, I self-sabotage, and my body responds in kind. I may experience poor health, overeating, reactions to others, and lack—in my self-esteem, relationships, money, energy, desires, hopes, and even dreams. With self-acceptance and love comes a different kind of creative energy, an energy which is open, free and peaceful. Self-acceptance brings vitality, wholeness, health, joy, abundance, and wellbeing.

Like a pot that's been broken into hundreds of pieces, I too, have become broken. I am in the process of finding myself—all of those lost shards. They are hiding away in the shadows to be acknowledged. They are waiting in dungeons, hoping to be called back home. Love is the glue. It alone reassembles the pot and makes it whole. Love for myself makes me whole again.

We all have dungeons. Mine may look different, but we all have them—lost boys and girls locked away crying out in pain. The key to unlocking the dungeon and freeing those children goes against highly engrained social morés. And that is the thought that we have to continually be better than we are right now. If there is one key that would unlock the dungeon, it is activating our hearts and emitting love to ourselves. Only in the acceptance of who we are now, and who we have ever been, will we truly choose to be happy. Only then, will we change our ways and do things better. It is the most spiritual thing we can do for the planet and for our own lives.

Let us heed this tale and open the dungeon doors. May we activate our hearts and emanate love. May we emanate love … unto ourselves.

Dedicated to my children and granddaughter, Jaden. May you thrive in a world ahead—a world of kindness and love, where you are encouraged to touch your magnificence and accept yourselves fully. May you also positively affect the lives of others and mirror to them their innermost beauty.

To my friends, family, significant loved ones, mentors and teachers. I thank you. I thank you for encouraging me as I traverse the many altitudes of my journey. Your brilliant lights shine upon me and have shown me my shadows, and often my way. The insights I have gathered along my path are simply invaluable. Thank you for so many things, maybe most importantly, for your loving me through my discoveries. My journey is blessed by you. I am especially grateful for my mother and father. Your amazing values and integrity were never lost on me. I love you.

~Tina Gibson

Make it

"to have joy you must make it.
and take it. saying you want
it isn't enough. maybe that's
with everything ... saying you
want it isn't enough. make it.
take it. know it's yours."

~ TERRI ST. CLOUD
www.BoneSighArts.com

Kourtney Hall

KOURTNEY HALL is a certified Workshop Teacher and Life Coach of Louise Hay's bestselling book, 'You Can Heal Your Life®'. She has studied psychology as her major in her undergraduate degree, as well as spent time researching relationship dynamics and bonds that keep relationships connected. She is currently taking the year to work more on her love for the mind-body connection, and researching how to become, and feel, whole. She is developing her business 'It All Starts With You', and will help many to understand that by changing our thoughts, we can change our experience of life.

itallstartswithyou22@gmail.com
www.facebook.com/itallstartswithyou.22.kh?ref_type=bookmark

❧ Breaking Free—You Are Not Alone

So alone, feel so lost, "why am I so sad?"—I just feel entrapped, I don't know why. 'Mantras, mantras, 'Kourtney, say your mantras ... breathe, breathe, 'Kourtney, do some breathing ... breathe in ... and out ... breathe in ... breathe out ... 'Ahhh, starting to feel better'—last time ... breathe deep ... 'let' ... and now release it out ... 'go' ... I am so thankful for these tools, for the exercises, the words.

Four Years Ago

So alone, feel so lost, "why am I so sad?"—I just feel entrapped, I don't know why. I have been crying for days, and I just can't stop. I don't talk to anyone really, and when I am upset or angry, it's a very overwhelming feeling. I don't know where it came from; don't know how to make it go away, or how to stop it.

I may have lashed out, overly binge drank, or turned inward to a darkening spiral that now becomes more and more negative as I listen to sad songs, look at old pictures, sit at the grave(s) of my passed-over loved ones. These things don't make me feel better. In fact, they make me feel worse.

"I want the tears to stop." As I put on more sad music, look at more pictures, and allow my thoughts to flow in an intensification pattern of negativity that augments my anxiety, it feeds my fears, and for me, turns into anger.

First Steps of Making a Change

I decided back then, when I felt there was nothing else for me, that I needed to reach out. I needed help, solace, someone to talk to. I needed a change. My journey has always involved professional help throughout my life. I joined a group, and eventually broke away from the horrid reality that was my life.

I have always dabbled in self-help books, and journaling. My major was psychology and I have spent years studying different theories, and methods that human beings can use to try to make changes in their lives.

Reflecting back on this point of my life, I became more connected with myself, but when the pain lessened and remained stagnant, my self-love work did as well.

My Past to Get to Today

Even though there have been moments in my life that I am forever grateful for and hold true to my heart, I have experienced a lot of challenges, and events that pose as life lessons for me. At a very young age, I experienced a loss of my biological father. I was twelve years old when he decided to take his life, and at that age I wasn't sure how to react. My biological father (Mike) was not a constant in my life. He and my mother split and my mother met my dad (Kevin) when I was two. When the words were spoken to me, I remember feeling fear, and sadness. I was confused, and a part of me felt void. Carrying on throughout the rest of my life until now, I have struggled with the absence of my birth father. Feelings of abandonment, and mis-belonging have been both personal, emotional, and intimate challenges I continue to work on today. I can reflect now and realize how this event in my life has had an impact on decisions, or life outcomes. At the time, however, I was unaware of misfortunate events and the connection to the death of Mike.

My childhood, for the most part was a healthy, happy one. Our family was dealt some struggles. My mother suffered from an eating disorder, and due to this left to go to an in-patient treatment program. As a child, I was innocent to the real reasons mom was leaving; I just knew that my mother was gone for an extended period of time. My relationship with my father was not the best growing up, and entering into my pre-teen and teen years, I wasn't the easiest daughter to deal with. This mixed to form a battling, unhealthy relationship.

My father suffered from an addiction to narcotics. My dad worked himself to become a police officer. During my late teens, my dad entered a downward spiral of his addiction. His primary choice of marijuana turned into a choice of crack cocaine that ultimately, publicly ended his job. He was defaced on the front page of our city newspaper, and this tremendously affected our family.

I was always very close with my family (especially my mom's side). My Nan was my second mom, my angel, my guardian. My mom, dad, brother, and I lived with my Nan for periods of my childhood, and when I was fourteen, I moved in with my Nan. I was there until 16 (when we moved out of the town we were in), however, when I completed high school, I went back to my Nan's to live with her.

During the first year of my undergrad, when I was 20 years old, I tragically lost my best friend in a car accident. I remember this day like it was yesterday. It was Thanksgiving Monday, and she was on her way to work. She commuted to another town, and ended up in a head-on collision. One of my friends called me, and said she was coming over, however, when she arrived she was with two of my other friends. They talked with my Nan first, then came upstairs in a some-what train-like line.

"What's going on, guys?" I asked, deep down knowing something was not right. Brittiny, my childhood friend approached me, … "Kourtney, she said, Codie … " … I interrupted her, "NO, NO, NO." The fear I felt at this time was intense, not knowing for sure, but not wanting to know either, as the words would ring true to every sensation in my body.

"Codie," Brittiny continued, was in a car accident, and she didn't make it … " NOOOOOO … the words came out of her mouth, the tears flooded my face. I ran downstairs to my Nan, as she sat in despair on the kitchen chair. That whole week remains a blur, but so near at the same time. That day, October 9, 2006, I had experienced the first close death to me, my best friend. My whole world was about to change.

I can't recall now what I used to cope and grieve through the next couple of years over my loss, but it would be safe to say it was mostly a mix of alcohol, bad choices, and the odd counselling session.

During my undergrad, after my dad lost his job, and reclaimed his life through sobriety, my parents decided that they wanted to move to Arizona. My dad, being the American, was to make this move first. Our beautiful home in Canada was sold and my dad re-located. This was so hard. My mom stayed in Ontario with my brother, our family, and myself, as she needed to obtain her citizenship. Our family was now faced with the challenges of distance.

Adapting to life without dad was difficult, he left in August, and I had started dating someone new that Halloween. I was smitten. Completely taken off my feet, head over heals in love. I couldn't see past my new beau, only eyes for him, and was insistent he was everything I had ever wanted.

Our relationship progressed very fast, and things started to change for me. All too soon I was staying at his home almost every night. At the time I didn't recognize it as an issue, but my own life became less and less important as his started to cloud into my bubble. Family occasions of mine were a huge distress, and an issue for him to attend.

I will never forget my friend telling me how he said, "This family shit has to stop." Even still, I made excuses for it. My phone became a fear for me, as whenever it would go off, I would be a liar and a cheat, according to him. I ended up feeling it was easier to just silence it while I was with him, in turn silencing myself to my mother, Nan, friends, and outside life. I was losing my friends, myself, my sparkle. My love-fogged eyes saw past the flags that were slowly rising up the flagpole, and I excused the actions away.

Shortly after dating him I started noticing myself becoming very ill. I had lost over 30 pounds in a month. My body was inflaming in my ankles, and my stomach was in continued 'labor-like' pains. I couldn't eat anything without feeling the aftermath of it. I did not know what was wrong. Constant fatigue, and pain was starting to take over, and I became ridden to his bed a lot.

I will never forget how I would mask my pain with Imodium to go out with him, or he would leave me helpless and alone in his room. On my 24th birthday I had become so weak my mom highly recommended I stay in the city with her after my birthday dinner, instead of travelling back. He accused me of cheating, and lying, and planning the whole thing out. I didn't even have the energy to fight back. I was defeated not only emotionally, mentally, and spiritually by him, but my body's 'dis-ease' was yelling at me loud and clear, and as I further ignored it, the more intense it became. By the end of March of that year, I was admitted to the hospital for a week, and after tests, blood work, blood infusions, and scans, I was diagnosed with 'Crohn's Disease.'

That week in the hospital I was overwhelmed by the love, support, and care I was shown by friends, family, co-workers, and many loved ones. I had so many visitors, flowers, cards, and teddies, my room looked like greenery. I always had my close girlfriends there, or family after visiting hours, or was on the phone with someone, as I allowed the medication I was taking to kick in so I could sleep. The one person that didn't show up ... my boyfriend. He claimed it to be because we were not together. Oh, what a lonely feeling—being helpless, and humiliated by pain; the one you want to see, and be there to love and support you, denied me of that. I didn't think I could become any more weak.

During my time at the hospital, my mom bought me a book. I had always been into self-help, and reading different writings, but had never been introduced to Louise L. Hay. My mom bought me the book called, 'The Power is Within You.' and in this book Louise expands on her philosophies of loving the self through learning to listen and trusting the inner voice. I remember starting to read this book and in it she wrote how,

> "If any name disturbs you, then substitute another that feels right for you. In the past I have even crossed out words or names that did not appeal to me when I read a book and wrote in the word that I liked better. You could do the same."
>
> ~ LOUISE HAY

I appreciated those words. They gave me a sense of individuality, freedom, and the ability to have my own words, something I hadn't been giving myself for a long time now.

Manifesting life through your thoughts ... loving yourself and becoming happy? I thought: *what a concept.* Sure sounded more positive than what I was living right now. I read this book very fast, I became in love with Louise's philosophies and ideals of life. It brought to the forefront a life that I had only envisioned in my dreams.

I became insistent this relationship was over. I was going to be free and move on. I would use what I had just been through, and my diagnosis with a permanent disease, as a fresh new start. A new me, I was going to not be a victim any longer, I was going to take control of my life again, I was going to 'LOVE ME.'

As my family and friends nursed me back to health and life, the pain I had felt started to become nothing but a faint memory, and the sweet words of my ex became more present. Before I knew it, I was back with my abuser, and at the time, life was great. This didn't last long though, and this time it was like the relationship went even darker than it had been before.

As I reflect now, I can't even imagine how I survived the chaos I termed 'love.' One night when we were out at his friends, not too long into my recovery, I was waiting for a call from my mother. She was in Arizona with Dad. As I was texting my mom, Chuck took my phone from me. I felt furious, and couldn't help but think in my head, "this is my phone, who are you to take my phone from me, and humiliate me publicly?" Before I knew it, my thoughts became words and it felt uncontrollable.

"Don't touch my phone," I yelled, as I grabbed it violently from his hands and ran from the back of the house to the front. I needed to leave — my heart was pounding so hard from what felt like outside of my chest. I also knew that I needed to take my car from that home, as I didn't trust what he might do to it if I left it there. Due to having a couple drinks, I drove it to my work that was close by.

As I arrived at work the tears became uncontrollable — tears of what I can't pinpoint. Possibly fear, shame, regret, the unknown, loneliness, weakness. My boss happened to be in the back parking lot, and he questioned what was wrong. I asked to call my mom. During my long-distance frantic call I missed about 20-30 phone calls in a matter of 10-15 minutes from Chuck. Texts were filling my phone, and before I knew it, he was standing across the street from a local pub I worked at — waiting for me. I was so scared. I didn't want to go out there as I felt it would be a horrible fight, and I was unaware of the results. After my boss denied his entrance by my request, the night got worse than I had expected. Chuck smashed the front windowpane of my workplace from anger.

I don't even know all the emotions that were flowing through me at this point — embarrassment, resentment, denial, fear, and loneliness. I watched Chuck, along with the rest of the night crowd, resist arrest and be forced into a police car on Main Street of the small town I lived in. The police came in and wanted to talk to me, asking me questions about pressing charges. All I wanted was my mom and dad to speak with. The police informed me I didn't even get a decision in the matter, and I was told that the Crown was pressing charges against Chuck.

"Pressing charges," I thought to myself. I was in fear of how I would be perceived by the small town population, the rumors, and how upset he would be with me. I had downgraded the seriousness of his actions and somehow replaced it with blaming myself.

I had originally planned to stay at Chuck's place, so some of my personal things were at his house. When he arrived home after his interaction with the police, he took my things and threw them all over the court he lived at. My personal things, underwear, tampons, clothes, straightener, medication, were all over his road. I was also slandered publicly over his facebook account for all to see. He left me a voicemail and threatened my Nan's house. My poor, innocent, beautiful, beautiful Nan. The police were contacted and he was picked up and contained for the remainder of the evening.

This was the beginning of what should have definitely been the end. From there on, our relationship faced having conditions against seeing each other — which were broken, by lies, deceit, and sneaking around. This was not the end of the visits from the police in our relationship, and was only the beginning of both my person and property being defaced, uncared for, and destroyed. I lost myself; I lost some of my friends, family, and co-workers. I never thought I had felt so alone. I also battled mini-flares and complications more frequently with my Crohn's disease during this time. I was 'trapped' in a world that only existed of me, but at the time — I was gone. There was nothing, just black, darkness ... a wall.

During this roller coaster I reached out to some community support groups for women in or recovering from domestic violence relationships, as well as, made calls to the domestic violence call centre. I spoke with counselors from school, read books, and attempted to journal and break free from this life. There had to be more, there had to be a light. I was destined for more, and I knew the life I was working to create did not align with the life I was currently entertaining.

In the past 2-3 years, life has brought challenges my way. I was given the tragic news that my aunt was diagnosed with a terminal cancer, multiple myeloma. For the last two years of her life, I closely witnessed her challenges, pains, triumphs, and ending. I spent as much time as I could with her, and tried to make times as joyful for her possible. I wanted her to know how loved she was, how supported she was, and how she was not alone in her journey. Our family became very close, as we all had the same interest for my beautiful 'Auntie D.'

My poor Nan had to witness another of her many close loved ones leave her side, during the same time she was struggling with a permanent bacterial infection that would only become worse. I tried to be a support pillar for her and my mother, as they witnessed the third of their six family members transition out of human life. In March, 2013, my Auntie D transitioned. I spent that summer in a blurred vision, influenced by alcohol and parties, to mask my pain.

About a month after the death of my Aunt, I started dating a new man from the town I lived in. We knew how to have a lot of fun together, however, our relationship seemed to be centered around nightlife and drinking. I was exposed to a under-circle world of drugs that I never knew possible. That wasn't me, that wasn't my lifestyle. I felt at times

I was watching a movie on Netflix. Was I dreaming? Could I not find myself for once in a relationship worthy of normalcy?

As I worked myself through my teaching program that fall, I battled with identifying with who I was, and how I would make my mark on the world. How could I expect a life of 'normalcy' when that wasn't what I was sending out to the universe? John and I are still dating, there is potential, but we both need to become more in tune with ourselves, our emotions, our energies, and our life's purpose(s). I still have work to do on myself, as he knows what he wants and needs to work on for himself. Life was bleak, and questionable, however, I still had a sense, a knowing, that I was meant to be more. I was to take my life into my hands and create love, happiness, and joy. If I were to do this for me, and love me, then my outside world would start to reflect this as well.

January, 2014, my Nan took ill, and I needed to bring her to the hospital. As mentioned earlier, my Nan was suffering from a lung infection that left her susceptible to other lung infections. My Nan was, and will always be, my angel. She was my best friend, my roommate, my godmother, and my confidant. I was always very scared when she would get ill. I will never forget that cold night in January when I took her to the hospital.

"Nan, you look very ill I think I should take you to the hospital now." "Can I leave my pajamas on?" she replied with her ill-struck eyes and feeble body. "Of course you can Nan," and I bundled her up tightly into my car with the blanket wrapped around her, and we drove off.

This would be the last time my Nan would be in her home. During the next three weeks, my Nan suffered from mini strokes, and pneumonia that wouldn't respond to the medication. After an emotional, scary, and sad, time for my mother, and me, we knew that Nan had fought as much as she could for us, and it was time for us to show our devoted, unconditional love for her. On January 26th, 2014, my family and I assisted my Nan for her transition to her new spiritual life.

My Nan was an inspiration to many. She was always putting loved ones, and friends of loved ones above her. She lived a fulfilling life, one that she has had no regrets about and she has made that known. She has left marks in many hearts that will always live on, and she has left words in her writings that will forever be read.

Awaken

I truly awakened after the loss of my Angel, my Nan. After my Nan's passing I found myself at a distance from the social networks I would have normally found myself to be around. I enjoyed the luxuries of home, and the distance that it had to offer me. I didn't talk to some of my friends, who I was really close to, for extended periods of time. I found that confusing and upsetting, but also now could understand and appreciate why the universe unfolded the way it did.

I was able to delve into myself, and find who I was. I was able to develop a trust, and a love for me that had been lost over the years of hurt, pain, loss, and grief. The universe was giving me what I wouldn't give myself. Due to this separation and reflection with self, I became open to seeing what I had shielded myself from for years. I became aware of friends, and other people, with whom I wanted to surround myself. I became aware of myself, and what 'Kourtney' really wanted. For years I had been stressed, upset, worried about the happiness of others, and if they were offended, felt left out, excluded, or barely sufficed. Now I know that I need to love me, and be there for me; and not only do I know this, but I have worked to master some tools, and methods to help me achieve this desire. I cannot control how my outside world may react to decisions, or actions I choose to take in my life. This is my life, MY HUMAN EXPERIENCE, and I am the only one held accountable.

That following February my mom and I went to Toronto for an "I Can Do It" event. During this time my mom and I were brought to a light that we didn't think was possible after losing our beloveds. While there we were fortunate to meet some amazing authors, and hear triumphs, and heartaches, that people endured, and how they searched within themselves to grow through them, and feel love, joy, and beauty once more. We came across a booth that offered information on teacher training for Louise Hay's Heal Your Life® Workshops. I knew then we were destined to attend.

That following May my mom and I travelled to Maryland for a week's training with 22 other beautiful souls to start finding the light, and ourselves, that we saw back in Toronto. We were faced head-on with our fears, our 'guilts,' our losses, hurt, and pain. We were taught how to experience these emotions, express them, and envision them in a different light. We were privileged enough to meet and befriend women who listened to our stories, and accepted our feelings unconditionally. During this week we were able to witness not only ourselves, but also our new friends emerge with a glow surrounding their outer bodies that represented love, peace, gratitude, joy, and a new perception. This glow represented transitioning through old hurts, fears, 'guilts,' and grievances that were set free from the entrapment we had on them in our present lives. Leaving the training we took with us tools, and an open mind, that we could use to continue our journey, and spread our light back into the 'real' world.

Since then, and with continued training, seminars, and reading, I have become more comfortable with meditation, and using meditations as a way to connect with myself, and give myself the time I deserve to love me. I have learned about visualizations and how I can use my mind's eye to envision the reality that I will affirm as my present. I learned how to release my anger, anxieties, and fears in a way that is respectful and true to me. I learned the importance of journaling, journaling for freedom of voice, to allow my thoughts to flow on the page, without control or guidance from my conscious mind.

Thoughts

Thoughts are so incredibly powerful. They are the routes to how we perceive, enact, communicate, and live out our lives. Our thoughts create the energy that flows through our body; our energy is expressed through our actions. If we are focusing on the sad, negative, upsetting, self-defeating thoughts, then that is ultimately what we will create in our reality. Our brain is not capable of understanding 'oh, Kourtney, really just isn't happy right now but she truly does want to find true love.' Our brains translate the energies that our thoughts chemically create. Think for example, of petting a soft animal. Your tactile sensations send the message through the neurons that you are touching something, and our brains translate it for us as 'soft.' When I think of awakening and creating happiness, love, success, prosperity, and esteem for myself, I know it has to start from what I am sending out to the universe. How I send messages out to the universe is through energy, and how I create that energy is through my thoughts. Love yourself, and be kind to yourself. Treat yourself as you would your close friend.

Affirmations

Once I came to understand the effect my thoughts had on my reality, I could understand better how to use my affirmations. Affirmations must be in the now. "I am living a prosperous life, I am love, and worthy of love, my relationships are healthy, whole and pure, and I am safe in my life regardless of what happens because I love and approve of myself." If I were to create my affirmations in the future tense "I WILL be living ... " my brain would be unable to understand that it is a future tense. Our brain lives in the present moment, so when creating affirmations speak, write, sing, and read them in the now. Everything you are creating for yourself is already happening.

Gratitude

Gratitude is something I use a lot in my daily routines. I try to start, and end my day with gratitude. I can't help but feel good when I use gratitude. I have never been a morning person; however, since I have started using gratitude in the morning, and appreciated my home, sleep, and rest, I feel happier when getting out of bed. At the end of the day, and as an attempt to try to ease my thoughts, I try to think of all I am grateful for in that day. Gratitude will always turn my mood around when I am feeling emotionally challenged. If I am challenged with a negative, frustrated, upset feeling because of an interaction with another being, I have now started to think of what I am grateful for about that person. For example, one time I was driving and the driver in front of me was really slow. I found myself becoming angry, frustrated, and reacting in a way I knew wasn't true to myself. I immediately turned it into a positive, 'I am grateful this driver owns a car, and they have the freedom to get around.' I instantaneously started feeling better.

In my short life, I have experienced many heartaches, tears, hurts, and moments that I once used to 'define' me. Whether I wanted to be stuck in a victim role so as to gain sympathy, or not wanting to face my emotions head on, or possibly another reason I have yet to uncover, I am unsure. I have, however, started my journey into the light that mom and I saw back in February. I knew then I didn't want to slip further into the abyss. I wanted to work to climb into the radiance that was forming the glow that I am developing. I am able to recognize the gift that came from my Nan's passing. In her transition she was still able to give me a gift, the gift of love, self-love, self-growth, self-acceptance, and self-approval. In what seemed entangled, her death had me in emotional desolation, yet in the same sense, these depths brought me to mark the beginning of my luminosity.

Fear, defined is: *an unpleasant emotion caused by the belief that some-one or something is dangerous, likely to cause pain, or a threat.* Fear is, then, ultimately caused by thoughts, thoughts create our emotions, and emotions are our messages sent out to the universe. If step by step, thought by thought, I can re-wire what I am projecting, then I am in the process of enlightenment.

Awaken, defined is: *rouse from sleep, to stop sleeping.* Reflecting on this definition, and my story, I was in a fog, a sleep. I was conducting the motions through life daily, but not actually engaging and taking responsibility for myself, for my actions, and for my decisions. I was not taking responsibility for MY LIFE. My life experiences have caused emotions within myself, these emotions have in turn created thoughts, and those thoughts have projected self-defeating energy into the universe that has coiled into a repetitive pattern with similar interactions, relationships, friends, and hurts. By me choosing to practice medita-tions, affirmations, visualizations, journaling, self-talk, and further educating myself, I am becoming more comfortable with being careful of the thoughts I allow myself to focus on. Continuing with this is changing the repetitiveness, which has been my life. I am choosing to become awake to my thoughts, and conscious of them; I am on a journey to self-love, and self-enlightenment. I experience challenges with my emotions, thoughts, fears, and worries. I now have the tools I need to help transition through them. My tools become more varied with more learning, and they become more specific with practice.

The more I grow the more I am comfortable with experiencing my emotions, as varied as they may be. I understand that I will still feel sad, still feel angry, defeated, guilty, anxious, and fearful, however, I also understand and am open to allowing them to be as they are, emotions passing through me. I will acknowledge them, but then make a decision as to how I want to handle them, work with them, and through them. This is enlightenment.

I want to thank you, Nan, thank you for finally opening up my eyes, and kick-starting my journey, thank you for awakening me, and thank you to myself for trusting in the universe to support me through this never-ending journey.

An Affirmation From Me For You

I (your name) lovingly embrace fear, anxiety, guilt, sadness, anger, and hurt because I know these are only emotions and they will pass through. I am always choosing healthy, supporting thoughts to support these emotions. I acknowledge my emotions and I release them. I trust in myself, and my life. I will make it through hardships, and become stronger. I love myself, and send love out to the universe. I am awake.

Sending blessings and love.

(Note: For the purposes of privacy some names have been changed to protect these individuals.)

Dedicated to my Angel 'O' Mine, my Nan, for giving me the enlightenment to start my inner journey. You will forever be and always are in my thoughts, and my heart. I miss you, I love you, until we meet again.

To my mother, my friend, who is always by my side, I am so honored to be taking this journey with you. Thank you to my family, my dad who has shown me the true definition of courage, my brother Kody for always loving and supporting me uncondition-ally, and friends who have given me an open heart. Thanks to my readers for engaging with my story. My hope is for you to find your inner voice to guide you to love, be love, and spread love. Heartfelt gratitude, and appreciation to all my inspirations, teachers, mentors, and guides during my awakening.

~Kourtney Hall

Tauri Hall

TAURI HALL is a Counselor Specializing in Anxiety, Eating Disorders and Self-love. She is also a **Heal Your Life**® Life Coach and Workshop Teacher. Tauri completed her Bachelor's Degree in Psychology, with a Bachelor of Education and Master of Education in Counseling. She is passionate about helping those who are suffering create a loving relationship with self and have a better quality of life.

Tauri moved from Ontario, Canada to Arizona following her dream to enjoy sunshine and nature. She is married to a wonderful man and has two incredible adult children, as well as, a beautiful 2-year-old grandson.

Tauri's journey of self-discovery continues.

taurihall@gmail.com

Take My Hand; I Won't
🐾 Let Go, Promise.

My awakening: letting go will set me free and keep me safe.

I have learned the damage of clinging and hanging on so tight in order to feel safe. In reality, it put me at risk.

"Where are you mom? Why don't you come to me in my dreams? I wait and I hope and I cry and I feel so incredibly lost. I hope you know how much you mean to me. I HOPE you know how much I needed you too! I wish I could have a *do over*. Where are you mom? Can you hear me? Are you with me? I wish I could hear you. I wish I could touch you and feel okay."

I had written these words following my mother's passing. I remember feeling overwhelmed with grief and fear that I would not be okay. My dad and brother passed when I was a child, my sister March 24th, 2013, ten months before my mother who passed January 26th, 2014. The death of my mom left me feeling abandoned and emptied of possibility for security. How can I possibly be okay?

Over the years I have grown tremendously in my pursuit to find me and to feel good from the inside out. However, the loss of my sister and then 10 months later, my mother, revealed a deeper wound: a belief embedded deep inside—"I am not okay without you."

I grew up the youngest of four children. My oldest brother was seven years older, my sister six years, and my second brother five years older. My father was my hero. In my eyes he took care of us. My dad was fun. He was playful and patient and his family was his priority. My mom was my anchor. I did not know how to be without her. She was my safe place, my protector and my go to person.

Losing Me as a Result of Chasing Security in Another

I didn't even know how far away from me I had become; I didn't even know I mattered. What I mean is I didn't know that my relationship with myself was the key to my health: emotionally, physically, spiritually.

I learned to turn around, face myself and say "hi"; to turn around and offer myself what I thought I so desperately needed from others—love, security, approval, acceptance, and commitment. I learned to take myself by the hand and not let go.

Consequence of My Inability to Support My Fearful Self

My father was diagnosed with a brain tumor, he died when I was 12 years old and one year later my oldest brother was killed in a car accident on his 21st birthday. I was 13 years old. Within a year our family was forever changed. My world was turned upside down and I had no idea how to help myself feel safe in a world that was so dangerously unpredictable. At least that was my perspective as a child.

In my attempts to protect myself, I began to seek safety in perfection. I did my best to eliminate all possibility of abandonment by creating a "me" to be desired, admired and loved. No surprise, my true essence began to disappear and I became emotionally, physically and spiritually ill.

Tormented by an eating disorder that destroyed my ability to connect, truly connect, with others and most importantly with me: I suffered. I suffered in silence because I was convinced that to expose the self- abuse I endured would assuredly result in judgment, and abandonment. I would come to understand that the silence kept me separate. Speaking my truth, I would learn, is a way to love myself.

For so many years I had hidden away who I truly was in order to try to gain the approval and admiration of others. Somewhere along the way I stopped living my own life. I strived to be perfect so that I would feel I had value. I didn't let others see the true me. I didn't ask for what I needed because I believed I would be seen as weak and therefore, not valued. I was exhausted by the pressure I placed upon myself to always have it together, not only have it together, but to be desired, admired and ultimately loved. I feel a deep sadness as I remember the insecurity I felt and how desperately I tried to escape that feeling. So driven by my fears that I sacrificed my needs, my health. So incredibly lost in irrational thought.

The reality was: I never truly understood what it would mean to be secure or how that would feel. I believed that security would be created by my achievements, and as a result be validated by the approval of peers, teachers and parents. Even though I had many friends, excelled athletically, and academically, I never felt secure.

I never experienced a knowing from within. I never "arrived." Instead, my need for security persisted and I continued to look outside myself for what I would later understand could only be found within.

My obsession with perfection pulled me farther and farther away from my own essence. I really didn't even know who I was or what I enjoyed because I couldn't hear my inner voice through the screams of fear and insecurity. I began to dislike, even hate, myself, but never questioned why. How sad.

My need to be noticed was fed by insecurity. I continued to seek affirmations that I was not just okay, but that I was exceptional. I believed that I needed to be "better than" in order to feel I had achieved; the problem was that "better than" kept escaping me. I always thought that I had to keep improving. The eating disorder became my safe place, but I never felt safe within it. I only felt more anxious, more self-hatred and more insecure.

Insights, Awareness and Understanding

Today, I see the eating disorder was much like an abusive partner. It convinced me I would be nothing without it, that I would become unattractive, disempowered and alone. It convinced me that if others knew about my relationship with it, that I would be judged and they would try to sabotage my success, success that was only possible while clinging to the eating disorder.

In truth, it would later be clear to me that the opposite was true. Partnering with the eating disorder created ugliness inside of me, robbed me of my power, and created isolation and loneliness. Living with an eating disorder dishonored my true self. I judged myself; I judged others. I would discover that it was the eating disorder that sabotaged my success: personal, and professional. How grateful I am today that this relationship was ended. I am free to make healthy choices without the eating disorder thoughts bullying me into questioning my inner guidance.

Losing my sister and my mom so close together has been overwhelming, and incredibly painful. It has also created an opportunity to become closer to myself. I have learned I am okay, despite my loss, despite the ache in my heart when I remember they are no longer here in the physical world with me. I know I have a choice. I know I can choose to be grateful for the gift or opportunities that may come from such a loss; or I can choose to become a prisoner to the grief. I now understand that I need to give myself permission to feel my pain, while also giving myself permission to heal. I had always believed that to heal, to feel joy and excitement for life is to forget, dishonor, disrespect and dismiss my loved one who passed. I now know this is not the truth.

Funny how what I thought would destroy me—loss of someone I love, loss of what I believed was my security, having others to affirm my value — has, in reality, provided me opportunities to save me. The most recent loss of my sister and my mother has gently and lovingly urged me to look inward and helped me to develop a deeper relationship with me. When I allowed the pain to be present without trying to mask it with accomplishments, I began to experience my true essence.

I Have Learned

Our deepest fear is not that we are inadequate.
Our deepest fear is that we are powerful
beyond measure. It is our light, not our darkness
that most frightens us. We ask ourselves,
Who am I to be brilliant, gorgeous, talented,
fabulous? Actually, who are you not to be?

~ MARIANNE WILLIAMSON

I now recognize my feelings of insecurity and fear as self-doubt, as not loving myself. I have come to believe I deserve to shine and I have given myself permission to love myself, to be kind and gentle in my interactions with me. I have learned it is safe to go inside and step into my own truth.

I have learned that we have the power of thought to create things, to create emotion and behavior that may or may not serve our highest good. Thoughts are often adopted, handed down; they are not always true. I have learned that I can choose what to focus on and give power to, and what to let go.

I now look inside without fear, but instead with anticipation of authenticity and insight. I recognize myself as separate from the stories

I have adopted about life, people and who I should be. I am striving to BE, not to do, in order to feel safe.

For so long I believed that my ability to perform and achieve and impress meant that I was in control. I have learned to release my incessant pursuit of something that I could not possibly ever have. I am not in control. I never was in control and that is great news. Perfection does not exist; its pursuit is merely a consequence of fear and insecurity. In reality, seeking perfection and attempting to control only feed the need to do so. I have discovered there is a power much greater than me that is working for my greatest good. Thank-goodness! I can let go and trust that it is all happening in Divine Order for the good of my soul's purpose.

Journey Back to Me

For years I didn't invest time in me; I avoided feeling and replaced it with doing. For years I was sad; I was lonely; I was lost. For years I was in pain. I believed I was in pain because I was not good enough and that once I reach my fullest potential, once I proved to the world I was exceptional, then I could feel I had value. I hated myself, yet had no rational explanation why. In truth, I was afraid.

It was through the pain of suffering that I made a choice to seek a way to feel better. I began listening to many of our greatest teachers: Louise Hay, Wayne Dyer, Deepak Chopra, and Marianne Williamson, just to name a few. I immersed myself in their books and in their audio CDs. Why? Because as I allowed myself time to absorb their words, their ideals, I began to feel better. I began to feel good. They became my safe place, as I learned how to create safety within myself.

I have attended *I Can Do It* and *Celebrate Your Life* conferences. The more I learned and incorporated what I was learning into my life, the better I felt. I had hope. I had vision of what was possible for me and, best of all, I believed I deserved it.

I truly believe that, as Wayne Dyer often says in his lectures: *Everything is happening perfectly and for our highest good.* When my sister became ill with Multiple Myeloma in 2011, she asked me to help her cope. She asked me to help her try to make sense of her suffering. I feel inexpressible gratitude that because I had learned from many admired and brilliant spiritual teachers, I was able to support my sister, Dawn Marie, and share with her their wisdom.

My sister faced her suffering, and her fear with courage, with elegance and with self-love. I know this speaks to her character, and it also speaks to the teaching provided by the wise and enlightened teachers of today. Dawn was loved through their work and I was inspired and awakened.

As my journey in this lifetime continues to unfold, I am finding my way back to me.

From Me to You

How often have you wondered: what am I thinking? How often have you asked: how do I feel? Do you make decisions because it is for your highest good or do you decide based on how you think others may feel or react?

How often do you take time to just be in your own pain without judgment or fear? Did you know that was possible? How would you describe your relationship with you? Are you someone you can turn to when distressed, lonely or afraid? Or would you consider yourself a person to avoid because you abuse yourself verbally, physically, or emotionally?

How often do you celebrate your successes, your abilities, your essence? Do you recognize your needs? Do you provide for yourself or ask for help when you are not able to do so? How often are you willing to just be and enjoy your own company?

We are all students in our own life. Each of us has lessons to learn, and as long as we follow our own path, not the path of others, then we will be presented with opportunities to learn, to grow, to understand.

I believe that we are here to cultivate a deeper relationship with self and the most effective way to do this is to love ourselves through it. I would like to share with you what has helped me find my way back to myself.

Spend time just hanging out with you. Plan to do things that feel good and invest the time to do it on your own. Just as you would need to spend time with another person to form a relationship, the same holds true for you.

Be kind. Treat yourself with kindness and compassion. Even when you don't like something, be curious about it rather than critical. Imagine if you were harsh and critical with a friend. They likely would choose not to be around you. You, however, cannot escape yourself, no matter how hard you may try. You are born with you and will die with you. This is the most important relationship you will ever have, the one with SELF.

Express. Share. Be real. Have your voice. Be your true self! Say yes, when you want to say yes; say no, when you want to say no. How often have you agreed to something in order to avoid disappointing or upsetting someone else? How does that feel? This is a message that you don't really matter and your desires and needs are not as important. This damages your esteem.

Take care of your body. Your body houses you throughout this lifetime. Treat it well. Provide healthy food and plenty of water. Move your body. Some people see exercise as painful. Find an activity that puts a smile on your face. Being active comes in many forms; find what you enjoy and do it. Dress your body in clothes that make you feel good. Clothes, jewelry, accessories can be a way we express ourselves.

Pay attention to your thoughts. Thoughts create things. The quality of our thoughts will determine the quality of our lives. What conversations are you having with yourself? Have you ever been in the company of someone who was very negative, pessimistic or critical? They tend to have a very low energy and can drain you and make you want to get away from them. Now, think of someone who is very positive, loving, open-minded. These people will make you feel good as their energy can actually help raise your energy. Your thoughts have energy. Practice focusing on the thoughts that help you feel energized and letting go of thoughts that create fear and doubt.

Love yourself. Give yourself permission to be gentle and kind and playful in all your interactions with you. As you develop a more loving relationship with self, you will trust yourself more. Fear will diminish because you will develop a knowing that, no matter what happens in life, you will ALWAYS do what you need to do in order to take good care of you.

Becoming your best friend opens your heart and creates peace within your soul. It is a beautiful journey. You will feel safe in your world knowing that even when there is loss, when there is pain: you always have you by your side. You need only *take hold of your hand and not let go! Blessings, Tauri xo*

Dedicated to my family in heaven: my dad, Arthur; my mom, Kaye; my brother, Danny and my sister Dawn Marie, I am always loving you! I hope to honor you by living the best life I can and by helping others to do the same.

Thank-you to my husband Kevin, for always loving and supporting me. Thank-you to my two amazing children, Kourtney and Kody for your love and your friendship. I am so grateful you are all in my life. I would also like to thank all the beautiful clients who I have worked with over the years. Thank-you for sharing your heart with me and inspiring me in many ways. Blessings to all of you who read my words and who take away something to enrich your lives.

~Tauri Hall

It's there

"don't wait for it. know it's there
already. don't stop to feel it. move
in its flow without thinking.
don't test the wind ... just lift
your wings—and leap!"

~ TERRI ST. CLOUD
www.BoneSighArts.com

Deanna Leigh

DEANNA LEIGH is a seasoned C-Level executive with 30 years of experience. She worked hard to climb the corporate ladder making tough decisions quickly, being a leader, and never lacking confidence to excel.

Her diverse background from Not-For-Profit, Corporate, Higher Education, and Governmental management positions, ranges from Director to Chief Financial Officer.

After going through a life-changing event, she purposely began a journey to self- discovery and became a strong advocate in helping others do the same. She is passionate about helping people, sharing her life lessons, and inspiring everyone she meets.

She is a published author, international writer, public speaker, and sought-after business consultant.

info@deanna-leigh.com
www.deanna-leigh.com

Awakened by the Unthinkable

Most of us can't even begin to imagine something horrible happening to someone we know, let alone happening to us personally. But, I'm here to tell you bad things do happen to good people. I'm going to share a part of my story about facing an unexpected evil, fighting for my life, and surviving to tell others my message. This is very personal and real. I will undoubtedly feel all these emotions all over again as I share them with you, but it is well worth it, if someone makes a change based on my story.

You aren't reading my story by accident nor coincidence. I don't believe in coincidences. You are here for a reason and you alone will know what that reason is. It will reveal itself in time and, more than likely, somewhere during your reading.

Please understand one thing up front. I will ask you to open your heart and mind and allow your soul to speak to you as you read. Your soul—male/female—will be the voice speaking to your head and heart. Being open allows everyone the freedom to hear what needs to be heard, to change what needs to be changed, and to awaken what needs to awaken. ~Namaste

The Break-Up

🍃 "Sometimes it takes a heartbreak to shake
us awake and help us see we are worth
so much more than we're settling for."

~ MANDY HALE

I've always dreaded the break up "talk". Gosh—after all these years of dating one would think breaking up with someone would get easier, but it is never easy! You're breaking up with what, in the beginning, was a hopeful relationship, but you're now telling the other person it is no longer hopeful anymore. For you, the relationship is over. However, if they don't feel the same way at the same time, then their feelings will be hurt.

After dating a guy for four months, I was in that very spot of breaking it off. I was slowing pulling away, but he sensed me doing that. I knew the best way to handle it was to simply tell him the truth. Make a clean and clear break. Even saying that didn't make it easier. My location of choice would be a crowded restaurant. It seems easier in a public location. Sometimes you never know how someone is going to react like yelling, screaming, anger, violence, or even crying. I have had men cry and beg before, so don't ever discount that option from a man. You simply don't know what will trigger what reaction from anyone. I wanted to be prepared for anything.

On my way to the restaurant, I stopped by his place to pick him up since he didn't have a car. I drove only a few miles away to our location where he was to repay some of the money he'd borrowed from me. He more than likely knew what was going on or what I really wanted to talk about. After drinks were ordered, I said, "In the short time I've known you, your life has taken a drastic downward turn. You got suspended from college, lost a job that you still won't admit to, you are working part-time at a bar downtown, and you're pressuring me to help you more and more financially. I have already lent you money for rent and food, and I can't do it anymore. I always have to pay whenever we go somewhere. You can't have a relationship with someone if you can't even take care of yourself."

He, of course, got a little defensive trying to defend some of what I said had happened and blamed it on outside things which were certainly out of his control. After a little more discussion, and his heart knowing he wasn't going to sway me, he said he understood the reasons I was breaking up with him. Then he said "I value our friendship more than anything. You are, and have been, a positive influence in my life and I don't want to lose that. I want to keep our friendship." Then he stopped talking and reached over for my hand from across the table. He held it and looked into my eyes and said, "I really do love you. I understand I need to get my life straight and I will. I don't want to lose your friendship. I honestly don't want to lose you either. I still want you to be my wife someday after I get things right again. But for now, please remain my friend."

Immediately the voice in my head said, "NO! You can't be friends, so don't say yes." Then my mouth opened to say "Yes, we can." What?? Did that just come out of my mouth? Seriously—I was having this conversation in my head as he held my hand. I pulled my hand out of his hand and placed both hands into my lap. I needed to say no! I knew it in my heart, my gut, my head, and my intuition was making sure I heard it loud and clear. Unfortunately, I did not listen to my intuition—HUGE mistake!

Common sense should tell you, and everyone else, there needs to be a period of time when there is completely no contact with one another. A cooling off period, if you will. This allows you both time to emotionally and physically separate and have time to heal from the breakup. It's a natural process and should be done without anyone having to say it.

I didn't know what was going on with him other than the fact that his life was a mess right now. I'd seen it go downhill in a few short months. What I did see over time, was a man who drank a lot of hard liquor, even just before he went to work. What I did see was someone who had moments of kindness, and then turned around with words of anger. What I did see was a man who worked hard at two jobs, then suddenly not care about working at all. These were just a few things I saw at the end of four months.

Bottom line—It wasn't up to me to fix his life. He was a grown man and he should be responsible, at his age, for taking care of himself and his responsibilities. A person has to be happy with himself, financially secure, and not dependent on me for anything. We are individuals coming together in developing a friendship and possibly something more.

Flight or Fight

"Whoever fights monsters should see to it that in the process he does not become a monster."

~ RIEDRICH NIETZSCHE

About a month later, en route to a long-planned, spiritual women's retreat, I drove him to the mall and stopped near one of the bigger stores on the end. I didn't pull up to the door, but into a parking space not far away. I kept the car running, but took my seat belt off. He turned to reach in his book bag behind the seat and unzipped it. I thought he was getting out some money, since that was the purpose of me even seeing him in the first place. Instead, he pulled out a knife and stuck it into my rib cage! He turned his body so his back was up against the glove box, giving him more leverage with the knife.

I said, "What the hell are you doing? Get that thing off me." He didn't say anything at first, but looked around the parking lot to see if anyone could see him. I kept asking him, "What are you doing? Why are you doing this to me?" He finally said, "I'm robbing you!" He looked completely different in that moment. He looked crazy!

I was in complete shock! My mind was racing through what to do and how to get out of this. The only thing I could think of was to try my best to snap him out of this craziness. I kept talking. I was trying to make him "feel" something to get him back to a normal state of mind. I asked him, "Why are you doing this? Take my wallet and get the hell out of my car." He said, "You don't understand. I'm robbing you of everything you own. I'm going to fucking kill you if you scream, try to get away or do anything other than what I tell you to do."

The tears started flowing. I kept begging him to stop this. I softly said, as tears streamed down, "Why? Why would you do this to me when you know how much this retreat means to me? I've worked so hard to help plan the event with these amazing women. Why? Tell me why?" And in that moment, he looked me in the eye and said, "I'm fucked up in the head." When I heard that, right then and there, I knew he was telling me the truth.

He was still holding the knife in my ribs when he reached down to get the roll of duct tape. He turned his body around and back into the seat. With the knife in one hand, he used his other to get the wrapping paper off the roll. He couldn't, so he put it up to his mouth to tear it with his teeth. It was in that split second that I saw my opportunity to fight back. Fight him or die. Either way I was NOT going to make it easy for him to kill me. I put my hand on the blade of the knife to pull it off me. At the same time I put my left elbow on the horn and held it down, leaning my body forward. He didn't see that coming! I looked at him as I tried to pull the blade away. I could see he was pissed and shocked. He dropped the tape and was going to ram the knife inside me.

With the force of me pulling it away, him moving it forward and probably the awkward angle we were in, the knife handle broke off. I had the blade in my hand and he had the handle in his. I think we both were shocked. I fumbled to get my door open to throw the blade out, while he leaned his body over mine to slam the door shut. But just before it shut, I dropped the blade on the ground.

He was furious! The look on his face told me the fight was on! I kept my elbow on the horn, tried to get the keys out and tried to get my phone that was on the floor. I was fighting him with all I had by wiggling my arms free. He was trying to pressure point a place on top of my left hand while that same elbow was on the horn.

He then began punching me in the face with his fist. I ducked my head down as much as I could so his blows wouldn't have so much momentum. He hit me three times in the face. I got my hand free—the one he was pressure pointing—and reached over to try the door again. This time I put my left foot out to open it all the way. We struggled even more. He was trying to lean over me again, but I was holding him off and inching out of the car. He struggled to get my arms back, but I got free and managed to escape the car.

Broken, but Alive

"When someone shows you who they are believe them; the first time."

~ MAYA ANGELOU

I laid in bed for days, mainly in the fetal position, under the protection of my big comforter. My mom would come in and check on me periodically to ask if I were okay or needed anything. My whole existence shut down. Every time I shut my eyes, my mind would replay what happened over and over again. I felt hurt, stupid, and naïve. To me, I must have cried a river of tears. I didn't want to remember what happened. However, I couldn't shut the replay off. Was there a clue? Was there something I missed? Could I have seen this coming?

It was horrible to relive it again in my mind, but I do believe it was a part of the healing process. I was awakened at some point with the answer. The truth was plain and simple. I didn't ask for what happened. No one ever asks for such violence or abuse. I got angry at him! How could he do this to me?! Then, like a movie scene right out of "Gone with the Wind" visualizing myself as Scarlet O'Hara standing on the hill with her fist in the air, I said out loud to the universe, to God, to myself, "I will NOT let him keep me in this darkness. I will NOT give him this power over me. I will NOT remain his victim. I WILL begin to heal." And I did. It was a slow process both physically and mentally. It wasn't easy by any means. Just like breaking up wasn't easy—healing isn't either. But it must happen in order to move on.

Here's what I know to be true

Without any doubt, I could feel the presence of angels with me that very day. Their presence was so strong, my intuition told me immediately that angels were all around me. Quite honestly before that day, I'd never been aware of their presence. I believe that people who experience a near-death experience, heighten in their spiritual realm and awaken within. Some people, I'm sure are awakened without this extreme experience, while others aren't. I wasn't one of those.

I still get goose bumps to this day, when I think about them. They say angels aren't here to change the outcome of our life, but to guide us to our purpose. I know without any doubt I was awakened for my very own purpose.

For me, this is the day everything changed. Even though this was a horrible thing that happened, it was also was a good thing! I know that might shock some of you, but I can and must see both sides—the good and the bad.

Here are a few things that I've been shown to share with all of you:

ℰↃ 1. No Co-Dependency:

You weren't put on this earth to "fix" anyone. You don't start out to fix, help or change someone! I have made this mistake before! It will not work—not now or ever! You don't want someone who "needs" you to help them emotionally, physically, or financially. It is <u>not healthy</u> for either one of you. The person you date should be self-sufficient and not co-dependent on you or their friends for most of life's basic requirements.

But let me say this, if you only want to be friends, then that is different. As a friend, you can help those people any way you feel led to do, without asking anything in return. We are here on this earth to give and to help others, as long as we give it freely, not expecting something in return.

The person you want to date should be happy all by themselves and ready to share their life with someone. You can't make them happy—that is an inside job. Once again—this is the co-dependency thing. The weight of always needing to make them happy will not make a good relationship. If they aren't happy on their own, then by all means walk away and don't look back! Don't fall for the "fixer-up" relationship. Please keep searching for the right person. You will save yourself a lot of time, heartache, and frustration.

ℰↃ 2. Honesty:

There must be honesty from the very beginning on both sides. You can't base a relationship on a false foundation. You want your foundation built on solid rock. You know what I'm talking about. Solid rock will not break. You can stomp all over it, throw a fit, throw things on it, but if it's solid—you can withstand the storm! Don't settle for anything less than that.

✐ 3. Set Your Standards:

Be completely clear on what you are looking for in a mate. Take some time, write down on a piece of paper what you want and what you don't want. Let all those thoughts flow out freely without thinking. Write whatever comes to mind. Once it's all on paper, highlight the <u>must haves.</u> The must haves will be the things you will not settle for less than. For example, if you aren't a smoker and can't stand your partner smoking, then a non-smoker is a must have! Do you want a man/woman with integrity? Do you want a man/woman who has the same religious or political beliefs? These are just a few of the things to think over.

One thing I know for sure is you must be clear on what you want <u>before</u> you date. Because if you aren't clear, the human need for desire will take over. You will meet someone and if they are hot, good looking, or say exactly the things you want to hear, then you are thinking first with desire. You are attracted to them physically and not mentally. At this point, you need to switch gears and think mentally. Start asking questions so you can get to know this person. Do they have the "must haves" on your list? Don't be afraid to ask your important questions. If the other person doesn't want to answer them, then there is a reason! You will know if he/she is interested in more than just sex if they ask questions back.

Desire—chemistry is a strong factor. Please don't misunderstand me. I do believe chemistry has value. Listen up—To maintain a strong long-lasting love, there must be chemistry on both sides. But that can't be the only thing you have! If so—it won't last. Our outer beauty will change over time. What matters long term is what is on the inside—our heart and soul is what makes us who we are. That is the true measure of a person. That is what you will need to focus on. I believe the very best true loves have a deep friendship first.

Finally ...

In closing, let me say it is my hope you have learned something from my story. Almost having my life taken in an instant has deeply awakened me to these truths:

- Don't settle for a life that isn't what you want.
- You must make your life what you want and not what others tell you they want.
- You must love yourself first before you can give love.
- It takes great courage to love someone without expecting love in return.
- Live every day from a place of true gratefulness.
- Appreciate the small things in your life.
- Let go of controlling everything around you, except your thoughts and actions.
- Every day it's important to be a blessing to someone.
- It's okay to say no to others. Do not feel guilty when you do.
- Every day allow time on your schedule just for yourself.
- It's not in having, but in giving that truly matters.
- Never allow anyone to set your value or self-worth.
- You are stronger than you can ever imagine—so stand up for yourself.
- Don't ever be afraid of change. Embrace it as a growing opportunity.
- When you go through a storm, you will come through it stronger and wiser.
- Always be YOU and not what someone else wants YOU to be.
- Listen to your intuition! It is always telling you what your conscious mind isn't listening to. Pay attention to that voice!

You have a unique purpose. Only you can find that purpose. At some point in your life, you will be widely awakened. Your awakening will come from a deep place and you will emerge into a beautiful butterfly! That is when your purpose will soar.

Dedicated to God, foremost, for giving me strength to fight and allowing me to share my story. To my angels for surrounding me in love and healing. And to Aubrey, Andrew, Adyson Leighann, and Dex— you are my greatest joys!

A very special thank you for my family, friends, and fans who love me with all my scars, completely support my purpose, and are there for me along my journey. Always know all of you are a blessing to me.

I thank God for every life experience thus far. I believe it has given me more compassion and understanding. My heart is truly grateful for all my spiritual gifts. My intentions will be in sharing my gifts.

~Deanna Leigh

We Begin

"tugging on my insides she asks me to dance with her. over and over she tugs. finally, i notice. finally, i turn to her. holding no grudge for my being late, she wraps her arms around my neck and laughs in my ear. it's time to dance, she says. holding her in my arms, we begin."

~ TERRI ST. CLOUD
www.BoneSighArts.com

Verity Dawson

VERITY DAWSON is a well-travelled citizen of the world, now settled in Barbados. She has appeared on TV and radio and speaks to groups on the mind-body-spirit unit throughout the Caribbean via her businesses The Reiki School of Natural Healing and Feng Shui Matters!

Originally finding fulfillment through the UN/World Food Programme, she then switched gears and created the first combined gourmet vegetarian cafe and 'new age' bookstore in Barbados. She lives and breathes the Heal Your Life® principles and, as a HYL Licensed Coach and Workshop Leader, guides others towards finding their true self.

www.TrulyVerity.com

Staying Awake and In One Peace

 "Peace—It does not mean to be in a place
where there is no trouble, no noise or hard
work. It means to be in the midst of all
these things and be calm in your heart."

~ UNKNOWN

Down the Rabbit Hole

I arrived to gunfire on the tarmac. Our tiny U.N. plane had landed with visual instructions—there was no air traffic control and all I could take in as we made a final circuit was Mogadishu's non-functional, broken down airport infrastructure, ghostly with memories of other times I had plied its frenetic spaces. Then down a few short steps from the freezer cabin atmosphere, to be overcome by suffocating heat and humidity.

The greeting team yelled out something with urgency. I did not hear the words, but ducked behind a plane wheel for cover. Then another shout—**hit the ground** (expletives deleted). I obeyed. This literal touch-down was a tangible landing into another unimaginable reality.

Once the barrage had stopped, we were assaulted by a crowd of "porters," who actually seemed ready to make off with our suitcases rather than load them onto the waiting vehicles. A ragtag convoy escorted us through bustling streets to the UN/World Food Programme (WFP) residence. I grappled for landmarks—after all, I had lived in Mogadishu for three years in a previous UN/WFP posting and had known it intimately. Now it seemed the city had crept up to the airport and this new infrastructure felt very alien to me.

And then, an introduction to my living quarters for what turned out to be the next four months. I entered the airless house and met my only other two female companions for a reality briefing; I experienced an immediate sense of wild panic and asked myself why I had foolishly taken on this assignment.

So the challenge was to settle into a routine where I could keep my spiritual life active, as well as attend to long 12-hour working days with a minimal lunch break, seven days a week for three weeks at a stretch, before being eligible for a few days of Rest and Recuperation in the Mombasa, Kenya, support office, when local exigencies allowed of it.

Pool of Tears

"I wonder if I've been changed in the night? Let me think: was I the same when I got up this morning? I almost think I can remember feeling a little different. But if I'm not the same, the next question is 'Who in the world am I?' Ah, that's the great puzzle!"

~ THE ADVENTURES OF ALICE IN WONDERLAND

I've not thought of myself remotely as a War Correspondent. Yet, here I am many years later sharing this personal experience as a UN/WFP Administrator in Somalia during turbulent times. It is late 1992. Siad Barre, Guulwaade, Victorious Leader, had fled Somalia the year before. Five clans are battling for control of the country, starting in each faction's traditional strong-hold with two main stake-holders in the south.

There is no central government, no active police force, no post offices, nor banks, hotels, running water or electricity, no traffic code. Think organised chaos. There are wild-eyed, sinister, non-partisan armed men, high on Khat (or Chat—coca leaf imported from Ethiopia), who hire themselves out as mercenaries with their looted vehicles, at exorbitant rates, to the very same organisations they stole them from. They also provide security to households. Buildings have been "appropriated" and whomever fought, and got, the property is now the owner and demanding vast sums of money as rent from U.N. and other international personnel.

WFP staff were lodged in what used to be the Chinese embassy and living compound—two buildings, lavished with silk carpets, inlaid mother-of-pearl furniture and plump, now dusty and dishevelled, giant sofas and chairs. Importantly, the water table, already low when the construction was completed in this area, is at this point providing oily, syrupy, salty water from its well, which has to be boiled to make it even remotely drinkable. I choose not to. But soon even that disappears.

A brave local travels the long distance down into the heated bowels of the well to tell us what we already know. The pump has burned out. A hunt on the black market provides the repair (and we hope that this was not looted from someone else's well), but not for long. The water table really is too low and the pump is eating sand. So we are obliged to fill the overhead roof storage tanks with water from an occasional mobile tanker, which operates from some still-working bore holes out-side of Mogadishu. At a price, of course. And gravity flow through old pipes makes keeping oneself clean, with long hair, in the sweltering tropical heat, a long, drawn-out process. I would shower under a slow drip to the sounds of bullets flying around somewhere, and hope that the already-shattered window panes would afford some protection in the case of a stray or direct fire.

Over-crowding of available housing meant that at times we had 25 bodies living in what would have been two, separate, one-family houses. We manage to accommodate ever-fluctuating emergency personnel by using sofas, carpets, verandah spaces, or by shoving more beds into the sleeping quarters; but the sanitary facilities inevitably could not handle the extra pressure.

An elderly, probably looted, premise generator provides electricity through the evening and night. We give blessings for the Danish "Captain," a veteran sailor, now organising food shipments in the Port. He manages to keep not only this piece of equipment, but just about everything else functioning in our shared accommodation. Still, now and again, we experience hot night black-outs accompanied by the longest set of creative swear words in any one sentence that I had ever heard.

Advice From a Caterpillar

"That's the reason they're called lessons,"
the Gryphon remarked: "because
they lessen from day to day."

~ THE ADVENTURES OF ALICE IN WONDERLAND

At the time, I am a relatively experienced meditator, reiki practitioner, self-indulgent "seeker" and long-time Louise Hay fan. I had thought long and hard about how I would maintain my spiritual practices before undertaking this assignment with my favourite U.N. organisation. Despite the challenges at the time, I had truly appreciated my previous stay in Somalia and I now wanted to help those remaining on the ground in whichever way I could. I knew it would not be easy, but the drive to be of service and back in the fray won the day.

What I had brought with me, in fact, was a programme to stay sane during the commotion. Little did I know the serious challenges I would be facing—to stay alive—never mind keep my inner peace in one piece.

My survival kit included Louise Hay's *You Can Heal Your Life*, a 30-day Tony Robbins programme, as well as my ever-handy *A Course In Miracles* (ACIM), portable mosquito net, string and a transistor short-wave radio. A trusty journal, pen, and two month's supply of bottled water completed the prep.

The latter was immediately turned into one week's cautious sipping at the old Nairobi City Airport, where our 10-seater U.N. plane awaited us to carry personnel to Mogadishu. I was promised that the cases of water would arrive "later" and my harried boss, having been busy negotiating with various Somali factions, smiled knowingly and said kindly: "My dear—you have brought too much luggage for this small plane." Having lived in Somalia in the "good times" some years previously, I knew that there could never be too much of any basic supplies … And I had done plenty of research, despite no internet help at the time, on the complicated situation facing the U.N. professional do-gooders in order to anticipate what it would be like on the ground this time around. Nonetheless, the cases of water remained firmly on the tarmac as we took off into the skies.

On the flat rooftop where I meditated daily, I fancied that there would be a lot of people in the world praying for peace in Somalia. I somehow tuned into Australia. No idea why. But I placed my energy to be an antenna to rope in anyone's stray or determined prayers for this warring situation to be resolved peacefully. Within three days, I noticed less and less gunshots sounding during the day and, except for the raid on our compound one night and an assault on one of our officers on the street, we had no more troubles of that sort until three days after I left, when the U.N. premises were broken into.

The Mad Hatter's Tea Party

The second challenge to staying in one piece were the working conditions. Keeping a large and important operation functional, with a minimum of infrastructure and personnel, felt distinctly like being an Alice in the wonderland.

One computer (MOS/DOS, hastily learned in three days at the Rome Headquarters in-between briefings, prior to travel to East Africa) one printer, plus a couple of semi-functional, electrical typewriters, broken desks and chairs, odd pens and pencils, were what I was greeted with, and expected to work with, to keep a country operation going. A costly satellite telephone system kept us connected with the rest of the world.

Spirit thoughtfully, and very quickly, brought me in an Angel and Protector. This giant of a man, unusual for a Somali, was a polyglot and a "fixer." He had previously been the driver of a friend of mine in ICAO (International Civil Aviation Authority) and was now physically portering heavy 100 lb sacks being unloaded from the humanitarian relief ships. Somehow our connection was re-established and Mardade became the man who could sort out for me anything which needed doing—money changing, and then counting the stacks of shillings (the rate at that time being over 4,000 for one US dollar), protecting me from the violent rantings of people knocking on my non-existent office door ("appropriated" of course into someone's home), and now and again finding the time to reminisce about the "old days." He also put me in touch with other local U.N. personnel I had known in my previous sojourn. They had harrowing tales of survival to recount to me. We all shed some tears over those who had not made it.

Although the WFP workplace was but a short 200 yards from a regular apartment block, now turned into the UN/UNDP offices, we were obliged to travel with the mercenaries and their guns, for protection. I soon rejected this in favour of using my legs, hazarded Kamikaze Korner (so nick-named by us—a crossroad without stop signs, drivers high on Khat) and a carnival Dodge-Em atmosphere prevailing.

In my hand, a modest briefcase bulging with USD 50,000—my daily operating "petty cash". Remember, there are no banks. Porters, service staff and workers up country had to be paid in cash, delivered to them through ingenious and creative solutions in order to avoid ambushes. Similarly, hard currency was brought in by any means possible from the Nairobi Support Office in Kenya and, to be eligible for translation into Somali shillings, also had to be pre-dated to 1990 and bear the words *In God We Trust*. Any crumpled or torn note was rejected by the money-changers in the local market, as also were $50 and $100 bills. The market was the hub of all commercial activity. Besides fresh produce, you could find just about whatever you wanted, if you did not mind that it had been looted to begin with.

Anything could be bought for US dollars, including important-looking red Somali diplomat passports, raided from a defunct ministry building. For that purchase, all you needed was US$10 for this souvenir of a time when Somalia had its legitimate place on the world stage.

This actually turned out to be vital when one of our regular short-term house-guards was injured in a shoot-out in our compound. The "hospital" only had a skeleton staff and no amenities, so we quickly shipped him out, with his new, unexpected diplomatic status and a borrowed photo, to get him to Nairobi for proper care. Not kosher, I know, but a young man's life was at stake and I took the responsibility of getting him through the informal immigration that existed at that time. I think everyone knew what was going on, but there was a silent agreement regarding humanitarian assistance. In that sense, the Kenyans went over and above duty, and I am grateful to say that our guard had the due care and recuperation he needed, paid for by us house-holders. He was shipped back to his family some months later, a little the worse for wear, clutching an x-ray which showed a large metal pin in his thigh bone keeping it hinged to the rest of his leg.

We were prepared to carry on in this fashion, improving food distribution systems and ways of dealing more effectively with administrative logistics, until BBC World Radio informed us that there was to be an intervention from the USA. Mixed feelings. Knowing the situation on the ground intimately, we wondered how this rumour could play out in real life. We all had ideas of how Peace could be achieved in this anarchic state. What about a stealth door-to-door operation where all the mercenaries could be relieved of their arms?

What happened, in fact, was pure theatre. The world's Press seemed to be lined up for the midnight beach landing. The Americans immediately instituted a no arms ban. Good as gold, all the law-abiding institutions, grumbling, applied the new rule. Even our care-taker mercenaries risked their status and put their guns on the floors of the vehicles we travelled in, just in case. But the rebels now had their way with the rest of us. It was a most fragile situation and not only the expats, but the long-suffering locals, began to feel the strain of being thus dis-advantaged.

Through the Looking Glass

To keep Awakened through all the mayhem, I went up to the roof-top every morning to enjoy the fresh moist air and to do some yoga stretches and meditation. No snooze button on this woman's alarm. I wore a one-piece leotard, enjoying the freedom from the constraints of covering arms and legs when in public. After the US Marines arrived, my morning quiet time was interrupted by the hovering of helicopters and I soon realised that I was providing eye candy for the lads! We got to waving-to-each-other status and I liked the idea that they could be seen over our area. Who could imagine their fate a short year later ...

In the evenings, after hashing through the day's events, or distracting themselves with board games, WFP staff disappeared into their various spaces. Mine was shared with a Canadian voluntary service person. Luckily (and synchronistically for me), she was into yoga and holistic thinking, hence we got on reasonably well, respecting each other's external, as well as internal space. So then time to take out the Walkman and spot in the Tony Robbins tape.

Listening to him, attending to the messages—Awaken the Power Within—brought me a link to my regular life, now feeling **very** distant, and a reminder of the Big Picture. I still undertook my daily ACIM lessons and journalled furiously. I knew that my sanity and survival depended on keeping my inner peace in one piece. For that I had to constantly put into perspective all that was out-picturing in front of me. I took the experience of outward anarchy as a symbol for the unresolved emotions within me, still battling to see whether peace would be victorious; or would conflict remain my fate. I had not yet heard of Dr. Ihaleakala Hew Len and his Ho'oponopono system (a Hawaiian traditional healing practice, meaning 'to make right, to rectify'). But in essence, and similar to ACIM, I had started to practice it by learning forgiveness for my past, as well as the actions of the people around me. Lofty idea, simple idea, yet challenging to put into practice.

I also set goals which seemed impossible. In fact, one of them was to meet Louise Hay! This came true some two years later when I undertook the Heal Your Life® workshop leader training. Another goal was to create a New Age hub in Barbados where I now lived. This materialised very quickly using my pay cheque as seed money for the first book purchases.

I am not sure how the others in our close-knit band managed their composure. I am hoping that the simple rewards of doing one's job to the best of one's ability, and knowing that one was helping dis-advantaged groups, made the risks live-able.

For myself, I learned that my spirituality was integral to who I was as a person; that no matter what was going on around me, if I kept my inner peace, I was transformed from an Alice in Wonderland, where rare events overtook her, to Wonder Woman where everything had a place and a reason.

This overseas experience had truly enabled me to appreciate the peace enveloping the tiny island where I lived, the gentleness of its inhabitants, the freedom to enjoy sun and sea in tranquillity. With these deepened understandings, I bolted out of the Rabbit Hole into a new phase of my life.

"Spirituality is not to be learned by flight from the world, or by running away from things, or by turning solitary and going apart from the world. Rather, we must learn an inner solitude wherever or with whomsoever we may be. We must learn to penetrate things and find God there."

~ MEISTER ECKHART

CNN provided the historical info through
http://edition.cnn.com/2013/07/10/world/africa/somalia-fast-facts/

Dedicated to my friend and life-time anchor, Nini Sacco-Grassi, who created the initial support for me to take sail from a safe harbour, my always-loving daughters who have uncomplainingly flowed with the tide, and my extended family who have looked after me each time I berthed a weather-beaten ship.

My gratitude to all the people who have filled my life and given me the opportunities to grow. My especial thanks go to Dr. Patricia Crane for her unfailing support and love, Rick Nichols for his levity and wisdom, Louise Hay for Be-ing an inspiration to model, and Robert (Bob) Harari for arriving in Somalia just when I needed an old friend and a quick wit for belly laughs.

~ Verity Dawson

Kisty Stephens

KISTY MARIE STEPHENS is an Author, Presenter, Life Coach, Workshop Leader and Certified Addiction Counselor specializing in Motivational Psychology. As a Licensed and Certified Heal Your Life® Teacher and Life Coach, Kisty teaches positive psychology techniques using the principles and philosophies of Louise Hay via coaching or transformational workshops. Kisty is Director and Founder of Sparrows Voice Inc., a Non-Profit Organization dedicated to giving a voice to the voiceless and empowering people to live their best life.

kistys@gmail.com
www.sparrowsvoice.com
www.facebook.com/SparrowsVoiceInc

A Sparrows Perspective

Stage

This is a true story account written by me, for you. It's the story of how I found a power greater than myself while on safari in South Africa. I know what you're thinking, and I was actually thinking the same thing. What does THAT mean? Well, keep reading and I will tell you how my epic safari adventure turned into a delicate and bittersweet battle between my physical life and spiritual death. How living with the Sparrows changed my life, and finally how healing with the Sparrows gave me a whole new perspective! Yes, Sparrows are little birds and some of the most familiar and common birds in the world. The Sparrows I speak of in this story are not little birds, they are children living with HIV/AIDS. Yes, I went to South Africa to live with the Sparrows, to work in a hospice and care for the dying. I wanted to work with kids and adults alike and Sparrows Village was a perfect match!

Dis-ease

My very personal and spiritual journey began several years ago. I was on the path to some awe inspiring self-discovery via the usual route; self-help books, and hundreds of afternoons slinging coffee with gurus who claimed to have answers to my problems. I took great solace putting pen to paper and writing my personalized mantra for living, as well as creating grand manifestos on a weekly basis. I had survived the divorce, the heart break, the abuse, the move, my childhood and finally, my addiction.

I had become so busy fighting for my sanity I realized one day I'd forgotten what the hell I was fighting for. The life changers were ALL behind me now. I wish I knew what my heart was missing, all I knew is I was missing something; a piece of my soul felt like it was missing in action.

I sought out higher ground. This meant more visits to the self- help section and countless in depth google searches for yogis and spirit seekers. I found myself looking to anyone or anything that would confirm my existential existence, to validate me, to tell me exactly what I needed to do. I meditated, prayed, did yoga regularly but nothing was coming close to filling the hole in my soul.

Was the great walk down under with Aborigines in my near future? Did I need to buy a ticket to Australia and prepare to hike barefoot in the blistering sun, naked, or, was swimming with dolphins off the Gulf of Mexico the answer? It felt as though the destination was a moving target and the journey was merely a carbon copy of all the days that preceded me. I was a great student, willing to do whatever I needed to do to become an enlightened being, to experience humility and find peace once and for all in my heart. I knew what was missing in my life ... the empty and often gaping hole in my soul was getting bigger not smaller. Meditation and yoga brought me closer to something but only ever left me hanging on the brink of great discovery. Wiki pedia was not the answer.

A-HA Moment

I was in the middle of a counseling session one afternoon and I saw a city bus pass by the picture window that read, do you have a connection? Oh my god! Is this what I am missing? Was this the sign I had been seeking? I was searching for connection. It hit me like a ton of bricks, in the head, one at a time. Everything started to unravel ... again ... I was in my bedroom, hands and knees on the floor, head buried in pillows sobbing. I was lost in the middle of a wonderful world. I had no connection, no connection to myself. I had a poster on the back of my bedroom door that read in big bold letters, "nothing changes if nothing changes" I laid on my back, staring at the poster, upside down, sideways, cross eyed, the letters didn't budge. Dear God, I thought, what does it all mean? What am I doing wrong and why does my joy feel like it's bought and paid for? Dear God, I know I'm not supposed to compare my life to others but it looks like most folks are a happy bunch. They have something I don't have and I want to know why you didn't give whatever THAT is to me? The tears started falling like rain. I lay on the floor for hours, crying and praying. I finally drifted off to dream ...

Joy Rising

This is where my journey takes a very interesting turn. I decided to pay attention to the "signs", the sign on my bedroom door and the sign I read on a passing bus. I realized that I could no longer hide behind the people, places and ideals that were holding me hostage. I had to let go, once and for all, let it go!

Time to clean house! This meant handing out an eviction notice to all of the ideals I'd been reluctant to give up. Everything had to go. I decided to do something I'd only ever read about ... I was going to South Africa. I had a friend that lived there and she worked for the Johannesburg Star as a journalist. I called and told her I wanted to work in a hospice/orphanage and I wanted to work with HIV orphans and people affected by it. She asked me if I was feeling okay and I told her I was feeling great. She said she could find a place for me to volunteer and I said fantastic. I wasn't even positive what a hospice really was, but, I was going! The next day I purchased a ticket and was scheduled to leave in May, it was March, so I had time to prepare. I made up my mind. I wanted to see more, feel more and I wanted to do more. I would travel ten thousand miles one way to do some soul searching 101. I was dancing with the stars, I was anxious, nervous, scared to death, and secretly I was so excited to feel this alive. I ... was ... alive ... again.

I was as spiritually fit as any one woman could be. I prayed daily, sometimes two or three times, meditated often, and tagged myself a "meta", which is short for meta- physical, lover of all spiritual theories that fall into the non-traditional category. Keep in mind this was before Elizabeth Gilbert, so at this time I did not own a copy of Eat, Pray, Love because it did not exist. This is my version of it and South Africa is my destination.

Johannesburg

I arrived at Johannesburg in the middle of the day. It was May 15th to be exact. I was finally here. In my luggage I had all of the things I could think of for an African adventure, khaki shorts, pants, army looking boots and hat. Few self-help prayer books, candles (in case they were out) some bug spray, perfume, and toothbrushes, lots of them. My dentist wanted to send something to the orphans so I had a case of tooth brushes in tow. Yep, I was going to make an impact, somehow. I was so relieved and elated to be on a different continent and far, far away from my average and crumbling life, I didn't even realize how tired I was. Ten thousand miles tired! I only had 100 kilometers to go, next destination is Sparrows Village my home away from home for the next four months. I was already concerned that four months would be too long. Wee bit nervous about being so far from home, I'd never left the United States, ever, okay I can do this I thought, must be brave!

Sparrows

Today started out the same way all my days began, coffee, stretching, playing with the dog and checking my emails. Kathryn, Sammie and I were scheduled to take seven younger children horse-back riding on a game reserve. I was looking forward to this day for quite some time because it was what being in Africa was all about, the wild life! Krugersdorp game reserve was our plan for the day. Once we arrived at the reserve we were lined up and questioned about how much experience we'd had riding horses. Well, I am from Nebraska originally and have ridden horses for years so I was put at the front of the line. Surprised they knew what a Nebraskan even was. I was given the most difficult horse and it went down the line from there, matching horse to rider, some riders as young as ten. My first red flag should have been they thought I was an experienced rider.

We started off on the journey. I was terribly excited to be on safari, even if it was with seven kids, two volunteers and three strangers. I looked out on to the horizon and it was so surreal and beautiful, here I was, in South Africa about to undertake a real life safari on a game reserve. Welcome to Africa I thought, this is "the bush" as they say. I was lit up from the inside out and eager to partake on this epic journey.

Safari

It seemed as though the horses were cooperating very well. There were seven kids, six adults and a fella named Dereck who was deemed our fearless leader. Dereck was also the owner and operator of Krugersdorp Safari Adventures. It was Derek who told us to be on the look-out for giraffes and other wild animals. He also taught a few at the last minute how to ride a horse, which can't be good considering we were really on a safari! Once everyone was situated and every horse had a rider we began to form a line. Took a few minutes but eventually we were single file and ready to rock! I was next to last in the line-up with only one horse behind me. My horse's name was Dunn, he was fairly old and ate a lot, so needless to say we traveled very slowly, I don't think he could have galloped if he wanted to so I felt quite safe on his saddle.

I was falling behind a little but could still hear Dereck at the front of the line shouting out the names of wild animals he spotted in our midst. The beauty of being on a horse, I was told, is that wild animals cannot detect the human scent over the horses scent. So in essence it creates the perfect storm, no detectable scent.

The excitement was building and the scenery was absolutely beautiful. Right out of a magazine, picture perfect, breath taking and serene! I was just starting to enjoy the trot when without warning I noticed two horse's running back towards me and much to my dismay the horses had no riders, where were the kids? I heard commotion and kids ... crying? Dereck quickly took control of the situation and put the fallen kids crying and all back in the saddle. Things were getting tense and fast. The kids didn't appear to be hurt and no one was complaining so we continued on the trail at a very slow and safe trot with Dereck in the lead and Anika and I heading up the rear.

In the distance I saw what looked like zebras, oh my, and a herd of what looked like wildebeests. It was exhilarating to be riding with wild animals at large and our horses didn't seem to mind one bit. We caught up with the zebras and soon were walking side by side, horse and zebra. I couldn't take my eyes off of them, it was so beautiful. It was completely and uniquely amazing how it all just blended in. I could literally reach over and touch the zebras. My fears were melting away and I was becoming one with these beautiful creatures in their element and I also in mine. The wildebeests were quite scattered and appeared to be a nervous bunch. In no time at all the wildebeests were upon our caravan and heading the opposite direction of the zebras. The wildebeests decided to move quickly and darted between our horses, this is when the trouble began. Several horses became spooked and started moving in different directions.

I was scared. My horse was doing fine and we were still just several feet from the zebras when it happened, several kids went flying from their horses again, and landed on the ground. No one appeared to be hurt, just scared, and rightfully so. It was getting uncomfortable. I could not really hear what was happening because we had lost more ground and were even further behind the group but Dereck started picking up kids and pairing them with the volunteers and adults. I had had enough, I was ready to go back to the orphanage ... panic was creeping in. It was like a scene from a bad movie and everything was falling apart, kids were crying and Dereck was pairing everyone up now, young riders with volunteers. Anika who was behind me on her own horse was now riding with me on mine. The horses that had fallen riders were all full gallop and moving in the opposite direction, riding off deeper into the Sahara. We had turned our caravan around, what was left of it and started heading home, wherever that was! A young zebra ran out from the herd and in between our horses. My horse reared back and I held on to Anika to steady myself and try to keep her in one place. These damn European saddles I thought, there was nothing to hang on to. I was formally scared out of my mind ... It was a series of events that led up to the fall ... black and white stripes moving swiftly on my right while wildebeests moved with great speed and grace on my left. Heavy sigh ... This was Africa and again, it took my breath away with its wild beauty. The serenity nurtured my own wild heart!

Falling Down

I made a quick decision to push up off of the saddle and try to land safely on the ground. I did not want to be thrown off my horse the same way everyone else was. So, I asked Anika if she could hang on to me tightly and trust me to fly off of a moving horse. She said yes, she was scared, so I wrapped my arms around her and we pushed off the saddle as hard as we could. It was a good push because we went flying out of the saddle into the air and final destination was the hard African ground. Plop ... I landed on my back with Anika still in my arms, so yes, she landed on top of me. This is when I heard the very loud pop, more like a bone breaking pop, it was loud and I wasn't certain where or what was breaking. Anika jumped off of me and ran away, afraid yet still of the wild bucking going on all around our head. The horses had been spooked and I was in full panic mode by this time. I was afraid my head would be stomped on because the horses were just feet away from my broken body lying on the ground. I was screaming for someone to take the horses so not to get stomped on. Please come get these horses, please, I was yelling by this time. I cannot move, something is broken, please help me I cannot get out of the way. The horses were rearing up on their back legs and whining and snorting and jumping, kicking and landing on all fours just feet away from my already damaged body. I was sweating bullets, beads were forming on my forehead that were the size of pebbles.

This was not going to turn out nicely. I was beginning to understand that I could not feel my legs, or my lower torso for that matter. Oh my god, oh my god, I cannot wiggle my toes, I cannot feel my toes. The pain is getting worse and fast, I feel like I'm going to pass out now from the pain, any minute. Panic was setting into my body as I tried to remain calm and figure out which bone I heard go pop then crack. Was it my back, my neck, was it my leg, my shoulder? I didn't know what broke all I knew was I could not feel my feet at all so I was guessing it was my back? Oh my god, do I have a broken back ... ? I closed my eyes to try to catch my breath and the first thing I saw with my eyes closed was Christopher Reeves, I kid you not, I knew at that point I was screwed.

Getting Up

Dereck, the guy that was supposed to be in charge of the gig finally got to me about the same time Chris did. Chris was the med student from the UK whom I simply adored. She was also a volunteer. They were both at my side asking me hundreds of questions to which the only reply I could muster was, "Chris, I'm scared, I'm really scared and I cannot feel my legs" Can you feel your toes she asked as she wiggled them and I said yes, I think I can, then she said, can you move your toes so I tried again, they moved a little. Chris and Dereck got on either side of me and said, "now on the count of three we are going to pick you up and slowly walk you to the truck." By this time Dereck had drove the little Subaru safari truck over to me as close as he could without running me over. What if I broke my back, what if I broke my neck. I was fading in and out of reality. I could hear the growing concern all around me but was having difficulty responding. It didn't make sense. Lying on my back with people hovering over me was not making any sense. Chris bent over my head and said, "Kisty, you have to get up because no one is coming to get you, we are in the Bush."

I closed my eyes and whispered please God help me get to that truck. I have never been so scared in my life. I promise to be the best person I can be everyday if you will help me get to a hospital. Even I knew enough to know that a person should not move if they have a break for fear of permanent damage or worse yet, paralysis. I had to get up.

As the two adults pulled me to my feet I instantaneously projectile vomited and started to fall back to the ground, I could not hold my body upright, too much pain, shooting pain, I was passing out and fighting to hold my wobbling ground. I fought with every inch of my being to stay upright, I could see the truck it was only a few feet in front of me. Chris handed me a soda pop and said drink this. It was the soda pop that got me to the truck I think. What was only a few short steps took forever and finally I was at the door. It was an agonizing journey and there are many more painful moments I could share with you but I will tell you that after three hours of being in the truck and driving through rush hour traffic in Johannesburg, trying to find a hospital that would take a non citizen was pure hell. By the time I arrived at a hospital I was delirious again, fading in and out again and so tired, I wanted to lie down and sleep.

Once at the entrance for the emergency trauma center paramedics came out to get me, I started to cry for the first time. I was a wreck and was ready to be in the care of doctors. The paramedics were at the door talking to me and reassuring me I would be ok. I was in so much pain and shock was setting in. The medics told me they were going to have to straighten my body to pull me out. I was so weak and scared and in complete shock … I don't remember a lot after this but I know when they straightened my body to pull me out I screamed a scream that haunts me to this day. They told me to scream, the medics said it's going to hurt bad because it's going to have to break again because you have been sitting too long. Oh god … I was so relieved to be in a hospital and even more relieved to be at a private and not a public HIV hospital. I got lucky again! I had visited a few of those public hospitals while I'd been here and in my opinion those public HIV hospitals are where orphans went to die. Most went in very sick and some never came back out, they died. So I was completely relieved that I was in a private hospital. The day was July 10th which was my brothers birthday, a day none of us will soon forget.

Sandton Hospital

The next day I woke up to a trauma doctor telling me I had a broken pelvis, two small breaks and nothing else they could see. Doctor said I would be flat on my back for a month and to move slowly because I had also suffered some head and back trauma, possible concussion and last thing he said was I lost a lot of blood. Doc said I was bleeding internally, so I asked him if that is why my leg was completely black and he said yes. Doctor left, I went to sleep, it's all I could do. A few fellow volunteers came to see me in the first 24 hours to get names of people I needed to have contacted in the States, you know, the "in case of emergency" please contact 'so and so.' I wrote down some names and numbers, bank information, pin numbers, anything I could think of. I was in a pretty sad state, unable to walk, no phone to call anyone, no one to come sit with me, no one was coming at all.

I was desperate to speak to my mother or father or aunt or sister. I needed to tell them I was badly hurt. I wanted someone to come and hold my hand so I could cry the ugly cry and snort and fall apart. Wasn't going to be a great romantic ending, this situation was grim and I was alone. I knew if I started to cry I would not be able to stop so I just laid there and did my best to hold a conversation. I knew I was in bad shape by the way the girls looked at me. I remember asking if I was going to be okay and Chris, the medical intern told me if I was lucky I'd be able to walk normal one day, no limp. She bent over me and said you musn't move anything, you must lie straight until your bones mend. I can't even describe the depth of my state of sadness, it overwhelmed me. For the first time in my lifetime I was unable to care for myself and terrified of what the future held. This was not supposed to happen, I was here to save my soul not kill it. I was hooked up to three IV's, a catheter, a call button, a remote control, a morphine pump and a window with lots of blue sky. Great.

God less

After a few days of lying flat I was getting pretty edgy and restless. For the first time in my adult life I stopped praying. I was quite certain that God did not exist and the reason I came to South Africa was to learn that God did not exist and there was no such thing as a soul, or spirit, or deeper meaning. In fact, I was now convinced that God was the enemy, an evil entity that wanted bad and horrible things for me. How could there be a God I thought. I came here to help people, to learn how to live humbly, to give back, to do something good and now I felt like a foolish American tourist that probably should have stayed home and bought more self-help books. I was pissed ... God Smod! It wasn't supposed to end like this and my journey as I knew it, was over. I still felt small and insignificant, no different than before except now it was worse ... I was broken on the inside AND the outside. I was having a grand pity party!

Visitor

I had a visitor finally—awesome, exciting! I had a visitor. It was Noni, a 15 year old resident of Sparrow Village, an orphan with HIV and TB. I had become quite fond of her while living at the orphanage. Noni was by far my favorite teen and she was wise beyond her years. Most important she was here to visit me and I could not have been any happier! She told me this hospital I was in was very far from the orphanage and all of the kids wanted to see me but they had no transportation or money to come. Noni told me she hitched a ride for part of the way and walked the majority of the ten kilometers to see me.

She walked to my bed, grinning from ear to ear, handed me an envelope and said "Open this, it is for you from the Sparrows, they miss you Kisty. It is very lonely without you and everyone is very worried." I opened the large and worn envelope. It was full of brightly colored hand-made cards, lots of them, all were written with words I didn't understand. Some made me giggle, some made me teary, and most of all I was grateful to have a visitor bearing beautiful hand written get well cards. To see my name lovingly and carefully misspelled in every language made me laugh out loud. What joy to have this gift from the Sparrows. Tears were spilling once again as I sorted through the dozen or more cards reading each one again and again. I thanked her several hundred times for coming to see me. I began to tell her how miserable and lonely I was and that I missed my mother and wished my family was here and I realized how lonely I was for company and on and on I went. I had a visitor and a listener!

Sparrows Perspective

Noni looked at me for a long minute, her face somber, her gaze intent, her large brown eyes grew serious with concern and she listened until I was done speaking. The next moments were awkward for me as she spoke of the many times she had been taken to a public hospital, sick and dehydrated from the HIV. How she was dropped off by random caretakers, not knowing if they would remember to come get her, or even recognize her name on a roster. I am a girl with no living family able to care for me. I am an orphan and we are looked upon as a nuisance and a burden, especially when we take ill. If you are sick with HIV or TB you are treated like you don't matter, like you are a bad or stupid person. Noni said, "You have someone to pick you up and you have a place to go home to so why are you worried?" "Why do you cry?" "You must heal first and someone will come for you, yes I know they will" "They are making a space for you in the hospice now and everyone is so excited you are coming back." "You must stop feeling sorry for yourself now and pray for healing." I asked her if she believed in God and she said she used to be angry with God. When she learned of her HIV status she was very angry and hated God for taking her mother and father. Now, I pray because now I understand it is man that cause our troubles, not God. I had goose bumps when Noni was finished talking to me. She was so "matter of fact" in her speech. I had no wiggle room, nowhere to go, no rock to hide under. She totally called me out. It was then I knew Noni was much more than my favorite teen, she was my teacher, she was the reason I was here. "Thank you" was all I could muster.

She sat with me most of the day. We laughed and we even cried a little. Noni was wise beyond her years and so willing to share with me her most inner soul. It was that day I learned to be happy where I was with what I had. I may have been broken, but I had to break wide open to let the light into my heart. Noni was my light and I the broken vessel. When it was time for her to leave she bent over, wrapped her arms around my shoulders and hugged me for a long while. I cried in her arms, it was the sweetest hug I've ever had. As she walked out the door waving and smiling her great big gigantic smile she said, "Oh, I almost forgot to give you this, a book from my house mum." "She said she thought you might want a book to read." I was touched again by the thoughtfulness to send a book, written in English even!" Noni gave it to me, I looked at it and instantly started laughing. The book was titled, "Mutant Message Down Under" Noni asked what was so funny and I said, "Oh nothing honey, thank you." When Noni left and the door closed behind her I laid there for hours contemplating everything up till this point. How could anyone have known I have a secret desire to walk with Aborigines? This was yet another sign that I was exactly where I was supposed to be and it was slightly unnerving to say the least. God wanted my full and undivided attention and let's just say that if you ignore the whispers of your life you will get a storm and this was my storm.

Noni came to see me several more times and a few times she even managed to bring a tribe of orphans with her. I loved those days the best. I could always hear them before I saw them, everyone could. The Sparrows would come running into my room, smiling and singing, bearing apples and flowers. It was a sight for sore eyes. Patients and staff alike enjoyed their frequent visits and they would often come in my room to see the kids and listen to them sing their songs. It was my soul food!

Hospice

The day came for me to leave the hospital. My travel Visa was about to expire and my original flight had left weeks before, so needless to say I was ready for the next phase of healing. I left the hospital on four wheels and was so incredibly nervous about being outside my little comfort zone because I was still unable to walk, even after 14 days flat on my back. We arrived at the hospice at Sparrow Village and I was greeted with a little welcome home party. It was sweet and I was happy to be there amongst the faces I'd grown to love. I was given my own little white room with a bed, a wash cloth, a water basin, blanket, pillow and a window. The tile on the floor was worn and the thin mattress sat perfectly centered on the old metal bed frame. I knew the room well. I sat with the patient in this very room just hours before she passed. I wondered then how many people actually died in this very bed. It was comforting yet somewhat disturbing to know this is why people came here, it wasn't to live it was to die with dignity. It was a motto at Sparrow Village, "Get up and live" and live is exactly what I intended to do, even in a place dedicated to the sick and dying.

It was a humbling experience to be doted on and cared for by hospice patients and staff. I can't tell you how grateful I am to have had this life changing experience. Having my wheelchair pushed out into the sun on a sunny day by a hospice patient is a gift greater than I can express on paper. The very same patients I read to, fed, and pushed into the sun before my accident were now reading to me, getting my linens and moving my wheelchair into the sun. I was connected for the first time in a long time. I was connected to these faces, to the stories, the kids, the simplicity of this life. I remember the first day I walked in this place. I only saw faces of people I did not understand, heard stories I could not resonate with and did things for people because I had a role to play. Now, I see nothing but people's faces and I hear their stories and I have no role to play. A place where people come to live out the end of life is the same place I found the courage and strength to heal my life. I have been humbled so now I can hear the music in my soul and the song in my heart. I sing because I'm happy and I sing because I'm free, I sing for I'm a Sparrow and I know he watches me"

Colorado

I lived in the hospice for a few short weeks before moving over to the orphanage side to live with Noni until I completely recovered. A trauma surgeon accompanied me home, to Colorado, he was from Canada and sent by my travel insurance company to rescue me—a little late but grateful for the much needed help home. As for today you ask? Well, eight years later and after many months of physical therapy, I walk with no limp and am back to hiking, biking and living life. Spiritually, I am changed forever. I live a more happy, joyous and free lifestyle with great appreciation for every single day of my life. Now I know what is important and it has nothing to do with money or success or copyrights or newsletters. The Sparrows taught me to be faithful to the moment, respect everyone … especially those I don't understand, and above all be gentle and kind to my self. Every time I see a Sparrow I smile and remember. When a child dies God sends a Sparrow to remind us how precious life is and to appreciate even the smallest creatures. Noni passed away last year from complications of HIV and TB. She was 22 years old. As I write this story I have Sparrows on my windowsill, they watch over me always.

We are all dying, every day we are one day closer to the last day on earth as we know it. Death is a beautiful part of life—do not live in fear of that which is inevitable. It is not the end but the beginning.

If we live long enough in this world we will have our hearts broken.

Our love affair with the world begins with a broken heart.

Be faithful to the moment.

I sing because I'm happy and I sing because I'm free, I sing for I'm a sparrow and I know he watches me.

Be happy where you are with what you have.

Dedicated to my mother Kay Stephens for being available to me every day of my life. Mom, you give me strength, hope and encourage me to be the best I can be! I love you deeply. And to Sid, for giving me every opportunity to be successful. Thank you for believing in me and loving me. You are the best!

Thank you to each and every one of you for bringing your own unique light to my life. Thank you Sparrows for your many contributions and life lessons. Thank you to my awesome and dedicated tribe for supporting and loving me always. Special thanks to Dori Eppstein Ransom and Liam Ransom, Kimi Camacho Jensen, Dr. Anne Hatcher, Amy and Guy Stephens, Hannah, Douglas Mendel, Nicco, and lastly, to the memory of my father, Jim Stephens.

~Kisty Stephens

Constance Mollerstuen

CONSTANCE MOLLERSTUEN is a Best-Selling Author, Workshop Facilitator, Holistic Wellness Coach, and Spiritual Counselor. She is passionate about working with Women, Teens and Young Adults. Through her work she shares life-changing tools which promote self- confidence, compassion, life balance, peace and healing. She enjoys inspiring others to live an authentic life guided by Spirit.

While living on Whidbey Island in Washington State, she finds great pleasure in making jewelry, creating one-of-a-kind antique garden art, walking at the beautiful beaches and parks and spending time with her amazing family.

Connie@holistichealingworkshops.com
www.holistichealingworkshops.com

Life is Filled With Choices

When you are living your life on auto-pilot, repeating the same steps each day, doing the same things you are accustomed to doing and thinking the same thoughts about your life and the world around you, as you have always thought, what will your life look like when you are 50? ... **The SAME** ...

I am not quite 50, but two years ago I did the unexpected. I quit a job that paid me very well; it had wonderful benefits and security. Believe me it took about 6 months for me to recover from this drastic decision. But when you aren't thinking clearly because you are driven by raw emotion and high levels of stress, all rational thoughts will elude you. Awakening has occurred on several different levels for me in these past two years. Realizing that I did not need to work in an environment that was abusive and detrimental to my health and wellbeing was vital in order for me to get over the guilt I was feeling. Did you know that you have a choice in all that you do? You alone make the decision to allow your circumstances to control your life. You don't have to continue to settle for less, you don't have to continue to put up with being treated inappropriately, and you don't have to live to work? It has been completely liberating to finally realize this.

Living On Auto-Pilot

My life has been a series of ups and downs, as I am sure yours has as well. With the divorce of my parents at age 12, I felt obligated to grow up faster than necessary. My parents had me when they were very young and at the time I was hurt and angry, feeling like my world was falling apart. Because, of course, you know everything was about ME. Out of all of the friends I had, no one else had parents who were divorced. As if being the tall skinny girl with freckles and long curly out-of-control hair didn't make me enough of a freak, this divorce thing took me over the top. Soon I felt like my life was out of control.

My sister living with one grandparent and me with the other, neither of us with our parents, left us both feeling unloved and unwanted. I would cling on to those I really cared about only to push them away as they got too close. My own health did not matter to me and I hated food. Slowly slipping into anorexia without even realizing it, I now know food was the only thing I had control over. Food sustains you and gives you life. If you don't eat you will die. Anorexia is for those of us who want to die a slow torturous death, making sure to really suffer in the process. It is amazing what lengths you will go to when you think no one loves you and you definitely don't love yourself.

When I was 20 I married a man I barely knew and gave birth to my son. With the addition of our daughter a year later, my husband's anger grew and his drug addiction continued to take over his life, moving from marijuana to speed to cocaine. He became increasingly violent and he abused me on a regular basis. Being terrified to leave, because he had always threatened to take my children from me, left me feeling helpless.

After four years, to my amazement, I was finally able to find a way out. I was picked to be part of a program that partnered with our local county government and I was given an opportunity to work in one of the departments. Being able to make my own money felt empowering.

During this time my husband met and pursued a relationship with another woman. This gave me the break I needed to file for divorce with confidence and get full custody of my children. A few years later I met another man and remarried. To my surprise he, too, had a terrible temper, he was abusive and addicted to drugs. ***Are you beginning to notice a pattern here?***

During our years together we built a business worth half a million dollars, we had a beautiful daughter, then I was in a car accident that changed the course of my life. With the head, neck, and back injuries that I sustained, I needed to relearn to walk, to talk, and to do other every-day normal things like get dressed. The accident triggered Fibromyalgia with symptoms of wide-spread pain, fatigue, and extreme nerve sensitivity, and eventually the auto-immune disease called Hashimotos Thyroiditis. Basically, my immune system is confused and is attacking my thyroid because it thinks it is a foreign body.

My relationship got worse and my husband's anger grew. Due to my own illness and recovery, it took me a while to realize that my children were suffering from the affects of his anger. Eventually, I gained enough courage and strength to file for divorce.

Living my life high on stress was the new normal and my cocktail of choice to deal with the pain was Vocodine mixed with a splash of Zoloft. During this time I met a wonderful man who helped me to remember the good things about life and to see that there was an exciting future filled with possibilities. I bought into this story for awhile and really enjoyed it.

My children on the other hand, had different plans for me. It was probably not very good planning on my part to have children one year apart. Because that meant they would be teenagers at the same time. I kept the older two busy with soccer most of their lives. They are both amazing athletes and excelled at the sport, both eventually qualifying to play on top teams in the state of Washington. The downside was that we traveled 4 to 5 times a week for two hours one way for practice and games. We did this for a long, long, long, long time. I did not mind, as I was homeschooling them and it kept them out of trouble for the most part. After the divorce I did my best to keep them involved.

Eventually as they got older, the sport did not have the appeal it once had. The level of competition and aggression that had built up inside of them turned out to be detrimental to their wellbeing. My daughter started lashing out on a regular basis and my son started to retreat to his room, withdrawing from our family as much as possible. I spent most of my time fighting with my daughter over *e-v-e-r-y* little thing. It drained all of my energy. She refused to be helpful and follow the rules. She yelled and screamed at everyone on a regular basis, which brought out incredible anger in my son.

Children learn how to be in this world by mimicking the behaviors of those around them. This is called learned behavior, and good or bad, this cycle will continue until you make a choice to stop it. The three of us went to counseling so that we could learn how to cope with the abuse that we had endured.

Next, I moved from unhealthy relationships to unhealthy work environments. Always doing what was asked of me without complaining and pleasing everyone the best that I could; even if this meant working overtime, working from home and taking work on vacation with me. For two years I performed my full-time job and all of the duties that no one else in the department wanted to do, even the duties my manager did not want to do.

He was able to convince me that he was in the process of reclassifying my position to include these new duties which would give me a very substantial raise. The logic behind this was that I would be already performing the duties so I would have the qualifications necessary to step into the new position. Over the next two years I sacrificed my mind, body and soul for my company. I played a major role in the implementation of our automated payroll system and found myself working all of the time.

When I was not working, I was thinking about work, and the amount of stress I was experiencing was unbearable. I began to gain weight, I had problems sleeping, I was always fighting with my husband and I stopped doing everything that I loved in life. When my husband told me that if I did not do something he would divorce me, I confronted my manager about the new position. He told me that it was held up in HR and he would check into the problem right away.

Two weeks went by and still not word, so I went to HR myself and found out that he never even put in for the reclassification. I explained what had been going on and they helped me to write up a new job description. Within 3 months I had a new position with a raise and retro pay for the last two years and a vacant position which my manager once held.

For the next six months the four of us in the department did the best we could without a manager. I took on the majority of the duties and began working 15 to 20 hours overtime each week. It would have been much easier if I did not feel such an obligation to make sure our department fulfilled its duties. The hospital needed its financials and it was my job to make sure they were done, even if I did not have any training or documentation to follow. These new skills were valuable and I did enjoy doing many different things each day. But, I did not enjoy the overtime or the stress.

Finally a new manager was hired and I thought my life would be normal once again. I was wrong. This person said that he was not taking back any of the former manger's duties, as he had a new vision for his position. He expected me to retain those duties and that they fell under the category on my job description which said "Performs other tasks as assigned."

Before I came to work there, all of the duties I had were split between 3 full-time positions, now it was up to me to get everything done in 40 hours a week. I jumped into people-pleaser mode and began my journey. When I asked for a few hours off one day I was told I was not a team player and would be denied the time. When I asked for vacation time that had already been previously approved, I was told that the only reason I was allowed this time was because I had paid for the tickets, but that I was not a team player and I would not be able to take any more time off for the rest of the year.

Even if I finished all of my work ahead of time, so that no one in the department would be impacted, he still denied me the time. I felt like a hostage, and what did he mean I am not a team player? As far as I was concerned, I was the **Team Captain***!*

When you live your life on auto-pilot, the speed with which you travel is predetermined. What happens when the computer chip gets fried and smoke begins to engulf the entire body of the car? It was a day just like every other day—meeting deadlines and scheduling events. The Surgery Manager called in a panic. She needed to order some supplies for a scheduled surgery and she was leaving on vacation in one hour and the vendor claimed we were on credit hold because there was a past due invoice. I gathered all of the pertinent details and began to research. Within an hour I had resolved the issue and she was on her way out of town.

I then noticed that it was 12:30pm and I had missed my scheduled lunch which was at 11:30am. We had just been given scheduled lunches the week prior. This was something that was new, as we had never been specifically scheduled for lunches or breaks. Most of the time there had been so much work that we ate at our desks while working. My manager was in a meeting so I emailed him to let him know what had happened and that I would be taking lunch now, but that I would eat at my desk, so that I could meet my next deadline.

He said nothing to me all day. Then, when I was getting ready to leave that evening he called me into his office. He told me that he would be writing me up for purposely defying his authority by missing a scheduled lunch and that I was the most difficult employee he had ever worked with. I immediately broke down in tears. Three years of stress and exhaustion had finally caught up with me. He told me to go home and that the paperwork would be ready for me to sign in the morning.

I cried the entire way home. I did my best to calm down and wipe the tears away before I walked into the house. Of course my husband could tell something was wrong. I explained what had occurred and he took my face in his hands and looked me in the eyes and said "I have told you for years that you do not deserve to be treated like this. Go into work tomorrow and quit that damn job." (Okay he did not use the word "damn," but you can use your imagination to fill in the blank.)

Making Better Choices

It was not easy to disengage the auto-pilot. Years of the same thoughts, patterns and habits create deep grooves in the road. As I pointed out before, we all have a choice to choose which path we want to take in our lives. Many times you get somewhere down the road and wonder where the heck you are. The problem might actually be that you were not consciously thinking because you were on auto-pilot, letting old, limiting negative beliefs and habits drive your destiny. At a very young age we begin to learn our beliefs from the adults in our lives. We are born with so much love and joy, looking to explore and try new things, to experience in the world around us. But then, an older and maybe not-so-wise adult imposes their beliefs on us based upon their experiences. Keep in mind, if they did not realize they had a choice, these beliefs have been passed on for many generations. Our parents and the adults in our lives were doing the best that they could at the time. We can't expect them to have done anything any different than what they were taught.

The abuse in my life took many forms; bad relationships, terrible working conditions and self-sabotage. I had to take drastic measures to gain control over my life. My hope is that you are able to realize the pattern within yourself, so you can make different choices instead of settling for auto-pilot.

So how do you break the cycle? It begins with awareness. Something that has helped me to uncover the feelings and beliefs that were hidden was for me to ask myself some pointed questions, then to write my response in a journal. Here are a few questions for you to contemplate: What is working in my life? What is not working in my life? What does my family think of me? How do I see myself? What are my 5 most important values? Am I living with integrity and connected to my values? Why not? If I could wave a magic wand and have the life of my dreams, what would that look like? What is preventing me from living this life?

Doing this process will help you to see what beliefs are presently controlling your life. Then, with this newfound awareness, guess what? You get to **Choose** to continue living with the same negative beliefs or to replace them with more positive empowering ones.

Our thoughts create our experiences. So, when you focus on the negative in your life you will continue to see only negative outcomes. But, when you focus on positive thoughts and things that make you happy, you will experience more joy. Being grateful for the things that you already have in your life right now creates space for more good to enter. Each day write down at least 5 things that you are grateful for and be prepared to notice the blessings that you already have and the new ones that appear.

I also practice writing and reading positive affirmations every day, several times a day. Affirmations are anything you think or say on a regular basis. Some of my favorite affirmations are: "I love and accept myself exactly as I am", "I am open and receptive to all of the good and abundance in the Universe", "I am grateful for all who come into my life, knowing that everything and everyone has a Divine purpose that enriches my journey", and "As an instrument of the Divine, I am here to serve."

The hardest thing that I have incorporated into my daily practice is meditation. Have you ever tried to sit in silence for 15 whole minutes and try not to think of anything? It took me a while, but I finally accomplished it. Some of the wonderful benefits of meditating are: increased immunity, emotional balance, stress reduction, lower blood pressure, promotes living in the present moment, and brings body, mind and spirit into harmony. Try this technique called **Mantra Repetition**: The relaxation response can be evoked by sitting quietly with your eyes closed for 15 minutes, twice a day and mentally repeating a simple word or sound such as "Om". If you need more help, as I did in the beginning, you can try guided meditation. I found that the CD's created by Kelley Howell were extremely beneficial and I still use them today. She incorporates guided visualization with sound healing. This is AMAZING!! You really need to try it.

Loving yourself enough to respect your inner guidance and discover what your true purpose and calling in life is can be accomplished by taking the time to slow down and nurture yourself. After I quit my job I finally took the time to do this. I don't recommend that you wait as long as I did. I am thankful for the lessons that I have learned and am blessed to have found a new focus and direction for my life. Living with love in my heart filled with passion and joy I now understand that I am here to serve. This realization has freed me from the bonds that had tied me to my past by permanently disengaging the auto pilot.

❧ "I am the light of the world. That is my only function. That is why I am here."

~ A COURSE IN MIRACLES

"Self respect, self worth, and self love
all start with self. Stop looking outside
of yourself for your value."

~ ROB LIANO

 "Every morning you have two choices. Continue
to sleep with dreams or wake up and chase
your dreams. The CHOICE is yours."

~ UNKNOWN

Dedicated to everyone; you are a Divine being whose essence is eternal Love. Recognize this and share willingly with yourself and others. Choose to be in awe of the beauty that surrounds you and find your life purpose. Follow your heart and let your light shine.

To everyone that has crossed my path—Thank you for being exactly who you are so that I could learn the many lessons that this life has to offer me. Choosing to honor my Spirit and live a life that is filled with Abundant Blessings and Love allows me to feel Deep Gratitude and Appreciation for you all.

~Constance Mollerstuen

Diane S. Christie

DIANE S. CHRISTIE, SPHR, is active in her relationship marketing company. She is an author, a licensed Heal Your Life® coach and workshop leader. She is passionate about helping herself and others move beyond limiting beliefs. Diane partners with people worldwide to (re) discover, claim and develop their unique talents, skills and abilities and to create abundant life results, in her business and in one conversation at a time.

Diane lives in Olympia, Washington. In 2011, she was a recipient of the Governor's award for Leadership in Management. She and her husband, Bill, have fun and experience joy through worldwide travel; spiritual adventure; and heart connection with all whom they meet.

dschristie8@gmail.com

 Rise and Shine!

🌀 "Who looks outside, dreams; who
looks inside, awakens."

~ CARL JUNG

*A*waken. What does this word mean to you? Open eyes and get out of bed? See an object and get an idea for another use? Read a book or have a conversation, learn new ideas, and decide to think anew or determine to be different?

According to Webster's New World dictionary, *awaken* is a form of the word *awake*. It means to 'rouse from sleep, to wake; to rouse from inactivity, activate, stir up; to call forth; to make aware; to become active.' Even just reading the definitions, how do you feel? Like opening your eyes, looking around, and taking action? Me too!

When starting to write this chapter, I wondered what could be the best way to share this story of an *awakening*. I'm from the Seattle area, steeped in coffee culture, and love going to coffee with friends. We trade stories of all types, laugh, and probe for insights. Hopefully, each of us leaves our conversation a wiser person. So, please just close your eyes for a moment to visualize you, the reader, and I, together at a favorite meeting place, excited to reconnect after so long. For our coffee date, we know that, as always, vulnerability is a theme of our friendship.

Time to get caught up on news, happenings, life. And we've decided to share an *awakening* with each other. Ready?

Here goes ... You may have heard, a couple of years ago, after having been retired from State government already for a year, I joined a relationship marketing company. Yes, this style of business is also often called network marketing. True, I've joined other companies in the past 20 years and never did much of anything with those businesses. No success to speak of. So, why join this one? The product works exceptionally well. I love the mission statement and core values. The people were, and are, terrific. The overall company culture of tapping into human potential touched me and continues to stir my soul. AND, it was definitely time in my life for distinctly more purposeful activity. The business fit from many angles.

To be involved in the business, I attended trainings and easily digested the information. Mostly, I did what I was supposed to do to spread the word about the product and the opportunity. I had parties, communicated with lots of people, went out with friends and colleagues for coffee and lunch ... a lot. The weight slowly packed on. And to my joy, many people became happy customers. Then about a year went by.

So what's the story here? Remember how being so curious is an important aspect of my personality? Expressing curiosity is also an integral part of my professional training. You know how I am, questions propel me forward in life and questions kept popping up. 'What did I plan to accomplish in the business?' 'Who would like to join me?' These queries spurred lots of thinking and discussing ... in my head and with my husband, sometimes with anyone who would listen. I sought answers. I knew I wanted to help other people by sharing and offering great product results. Oh my gosh, I loved the smile on people's faces and in their voices when customers or prospective customers described their product experiences and outcomes. On the other hand, I had many reactive, negative thoughts about people. Thoughts like 'She didn't tell the truth about what she wanted' or 'He's worried about being a guy and guys don't do skin care' or 'When will s/he return my call?' At those moments, actually many moments, business life felt like it was happening _to_ me, almost like I was victimized by external events, other people's decisions.

🎴 "Obstacles are those frightful things you see
when you take your eyes off your goal."

~ HENRY FORD

Okay, I admit I was annoyed and unhappy. The barriers were invisible, yet felt so real. I whined a bit, maybe a fair amount, actually. I asked more questions of others and kept asking more questions of myself. Around and around. I like focused action and instead was confused on direction. I had 'issues', as the saying goes. When were things going to happen _for_ me? I wanted more people in the business with me. In my heart, I knew the business and I could both feel happier, more fun and joyous. The twinkle in my eyes had gone missing.

It was challenging to _admit_ I could use some help in getting to the root of unhappiness and dissatisfaction. Yes, there was THAT realization ... I could use help for an _eye-opener, an a-ha moment._ Open eyes, look around, seek feedback. Sound familiar to you?

🎴 "You can't depend on your eyes when
your imagination is out of focus."

~ MARK TWAIN

Then the back and forth bantering in my mind ... I felt like I was walking a mental tightrope! Lots of tension in knowing I needed _something_. Doing _something else_ was the courageous next step. No more hanging in an awkward balance. It was definitely time to stop berating myself for feeling like a failure. Time to stop analyzing other's actions. Time to step out of a heavy, deep, and real fog. It was time to light a fire, grab that invisible prism to look for another perspective. Grace and ease appealed strongly to me.

How to resolve this provocative dilemma? I had surrendered to the idea of asking for and accepting help, adjusting my view. Clearly, it was time to reach out and determinedly call forth a different experience. Help was close by, as it usually is. Grrrr ... I phoned Brenda Lee, our fearless and enthusiastic business leader. I asked if we could meet for coffee. She fearlessly agreed. We sat, I talked. Yes, I whined and mixed whining in with confusion ... or maybe whining IS confusion, barely in disguise. I told her that I thought I knew what I was doing. Yet, I inherently knew the business could work better. *How could I work better?* Perhaps the conversation sounded circular to her. I never asked.

Brenda Lee asked clarifying questions. She looked at me, her eyes focused, and listened intently. And she listened more. When I stopped talking, she leaned in and looked me square in the eye. Then she calmly said "I think you just need to get out of your own way."

Stunned silence. More silence. I knew, she knew, the truth had just been spoken. Then peals of laughter erupted. Confusion melted away. I felt relief. A breakthrough occurred. 'IT' was right there all along. Our interaction was a masterful demonstration of the fact and idea that we, as humans, have two ears and one mouth ... to listen twice as much as we speak. Right then, it felt as if I had fully accepted the Universe's invitation to recalibrate my life. Wow.

Are you familiar with mirror work? I learned mirror work from Louise Hay's teachings in her book, *You Can Heal Your Life*. From that book, Chapter Six, is a short paragraph:

❧ "Mirrors reflect back to us our feelings about ourselves. They show us clearly the areas to be changed if we want to have a joyous, fulfilling life."

A revealing aspect of mirroring is that mirrors are not limited to images in reflective, shiny glass. Mirrors can be other people, life circumstances, a passage from a book that provokes a reaction, and more. Usually, what occurs in mirroring is a moment of recognition that touches the heart. I'd experienced a mirror moment that was quite revealing. Next step for me was actually looking in a glass mirror. There, I *recognized* resistance, a fear, to looking deeper within me. I saw 'qualities' in me that I did not like and yet criticized in others. Hmmmm. Talk about self sabotage! AND, then I asked self 'Why be afraid that someone would say 'no' to me about my business? Would I live if someone said 'no'? Yep!

I saw and felt joy and excitement *around* me from my peers. The new question was, 'How do I experience joy *within* me right now?' Clearly, I had some important self work to do, from the inside out, to course correct. Time to stop struggling.

❧ "When I stop struggling, I float. It's the law."

~ FACEBOOK POST, JULY, 2014

I knew that words had no meaning until I chose the meaning. I am accountable for my thoughts and actions. Ok, I sighed a deep sigh and shed a tiny tear. No more resistance I decided. I changed my relationship with fear right then.

🎋 "Have patience with all things, but
first of all with yourself."

~ WILLIAM JAMES

Onward. Before bed each night and first thing in the morning, I looked at myself in the bathroom mirror and repeatedly stated the affirmation 'I am willing to change.' Nothing about '*to what*.' It was an opening of heart and mind together, to just be willing. Insights came, light bulbs lighted. I was patient with myself and quite audibly repeated a favorite, powerful affirmation from Louise Hay. "It's only a thought and a thought can be changed."

What next? Aha … I *changed* my thinking to what was possible. Then took some action steps. I *set* an intention, a purposeful thought to enjoy each and every experience and interaction with others. I *chose* powerful, life-enhancing thoughts and words and *decided* to believe that I could learn from each person. I *visualized* a circle of light around me and everyone. Where there is light, darkness cannot exist.

What were the changes I made? Here are a few, so far:

- Meet people where they are. Not where I think they 'should' be in their thought processes and in their lives.
- Use my ears twice as much as my mouth. (Duct tape is valuable!). Listen more deeply. Gain clarity of circumstances, points of view. There's opportunity to learn here.
- Seek that point of connection. There is always a sparkle below the surface in a conversation that can change the course of an individual's life history. Gently find it.
- Be open to feedback. Be coachable. Boundaries are not limitations.

This story has no specific ending. As long as I am alive, the *awakening* is ongoing. '*I am willing to change*' is my mantra. I believe my personal life and business life really are one and the same. Opinions, beliefs, and attitudes that are results of life experiences show up in both arenas, always. No hiding in the shadows. How I live in one arena is how I live in the other ... like two overlapping circles, and both are parts of one large circle ... my life. Aligned with this belief is knowing that the results of lessons learned in one arena apply in the other, don't they? I believe this state of being is true for us all. My goal is that these two overlapping circles are as close together as possible, always.

> "Life is a process and your participation
> is required. Just show up."
>
> ~ DEBORAH MORI

Recently, while looking through notes of a personal growth program from a couple of years ago, I found the life purpose statement I had written. Through a new lens, I re-read the purpose statement. I *re-awakened* to the power of the sentiment and energy in the words. Here they are:

> "I inspire and conspire with others to discover
> and claim prosperity, in ALL forms."

How do I show up now? I take focused action on and radiate my purpose statement, daily. As I grow, so does my business, in harmony with purpose. Each moment of each day is a new awakening ... an opportunity to bask in the sunshine of life and help brighten other's lives. And my life results are wonderfully different today as I demonstrate authentic willingness to learn and embrace the learning. Lots more fun, laughter, and serenity, for me AND those around me. Wow. Joy is being on solid ground again, in balance, and starring in my own life. And you know what else? I'm dreaming again about what is possible for my life.

Thanks for listening. Ready for another cup? It's your opportunity now. Please share. I'm curious to learn what's been happening for you. How are you getting out of your own way?

To Brenda Lee Gallatin, 2 star and rising, National Marketing Director ... Oh my, thank you for listening so carefully and for our conversation that day, for speaking the truth. Thank you for your ongoing enthusiasm, support and guidance.

To family, friends, and life teachers of then and now ... wherever in the Universe you are. Your insights and sharing of your lives awaken the humanity in us all and bring joy to the world. In gratitude 5GN ... Terry, Diane, Mary Ellen, and Linda. Love you, Bill ... your heart always shows.

~Diane S. Christie

Angela Serna

ANGELA SERNA is a *Professional Life Coach, Workshop Leader, Seminar Facilitator & Yoga Instructor.* She inspires people to live happier, healthier, and more successful lives through life coaching, workshops and Yoga. This work is her passion. She helps individuals create change in their life by uncovering the mindset that limits success in their relationships, career, health and prosperity. Using simple, yet powerful, techniques, she guides people toward a realization of their own power, inner wisdom and strengths. She also teaches Stress Management in the Workplace and has a great passion for the Conscious Parenting Workshops that she leads.

Angela@AngelaSerna.com
www.AngelaSerna.com

 Lessons In Life

Speaking my truth and giving up my need for other people's approval has been one of the greatest and most difficult lessons that I've learned, but has been one of the most freeing things in life. Learning how to speak your truth and learning how to speak up for what feels right and true for you—even when it goes against what the majority thinks and knowing that you might be judged for it—is crucial. Always speak your truth, and speak it in a kind and loving manner. Society teaches us to be concerned about what everyone thinks of us and, by nature, we want to be accepted and loved but sometimes we confuse being accepted by social groups and fitting in as being loved. If you were raised with the belief that keeping quiet and pleasing others was all part of keeping the peace and living a peaceful life, there is great freedom in learning how to speak your truth and no longer seeking others' approval. Giving up the need for others' approval is key to having true confidence in yourself and high self-esteem.

Louise Hay's teachings taught me just that, learning to love myself was one of the most significant things that I learned from her teachings. Society teaches us that this is selfish to love ourselves and that we must always put others first; I learned, that we cannot love others until we love ourselves first. Once you learn to love and accept yourself just as you are, you won't have to be the perfect size, have the perfect job, drive the perfect car, wear the perfect outfits, date who society thinks is perfect; nor do you have to do these things *before* you can love and accept yourself just as you are.

I know this is true because I did all of it. At one time I was thin and wore the latest fashions — I had a terrific job, made great money, drove a BMW, dated a guy that everyone thought was perfect and had society's approval from every angle, most people that I worked with labeled me as being a very confident and independent person because I met all of my quotas and maxed out on all of my bonuses. But I figured out that during this time I wasn't confident at all—I was operating from EGO. When we operate from EGO there are a lot of underlying insecurities that are mislabeled as being confident. One of the things that was interesting to me was that when I was operating from the place of ego, my ego was easily shattered, and it could be hurt by what someone said or thought. I was constantly worried about what others thought and did not speak my truth, if I thought I would be judged in any way.

With the picture of my life as I just described it, it appeared to be great, but there is nothing great about needing others' approval, there was nothing great about not being able to speak my truth because of being afraid that society would judge me. And at that time I didn't even know what my truth was, much less knowing how to speak it.

How often do we take on society's beliefs to fit in? When I learned to give up the need for others' approval, and learned how to love and accept myself exactly as I was, this is where I found myself, this is where true happiness comes from, "within". When I learned the power of the mind and how powerful affirmations are, it changed my life and I was able to build true self confidence within me. This knowledge changed my life, this changed how I looked at life, it changed how I looked at the world. I saw so many situations differently. People saw me differently. People who have true self confidence can do anything. As much as I worried about what others thought about me, I was also judging them. As much as I was judging others, I was also judging myself.

I built my self-confidence by flipping the negative thought patterns to positive ones by using affirmations. One of my favorites is, "I Love and Accept myself exactly as I am, therefore others Love and Accept who I am and what I do." Also, here's a very powerful quote from Louise Hay "Everyone is doing the best that they know how with the knowledge, consciousness and understanding that they have in that moment." This helped me tremendously and I would remind myself of this because it taught me to be a more compassionate person and to not judge others' behaviors. We have no idea what is going on with others. We have no idea what event has taken place or what experience caused their behavior or caused them to respond or react in a particular manner. When we know better, we do better.

 "Truth is not something outside to be discovered, it is something inside to be realized."

~ OSHO

Another life-changing experience for me was when I learned that our entire belief system clearly does form our entire reality—what we believe creates the world around us, how we look at things, our total perception of things manifest our reality. I had read many books and had heard this concept for a very long time. There was a time that I truly believed that this worked for others or there certainly would not be so many books and resources about this concept, I just had no idea how to make it work for me. It was frustrating to hear others share their stories; I thought I was thinking positive, I thought I was a pretty positive person, but it wasn't until I actually started using affirmations that I was able to create real change in my world. Affirmations and taking my gratitude to a whole new level was what worked for me and this was one of the simplest things that I had ever done to establish change; it's the feeling and enthusiasm that is put into motion behind

169

the affirmations that bring them to life! Putting EMOTION into your affirmation is the power behind making them work.

🌀 "Emotion is energy in motion"

"Nothing happens till something moves"

~ TWO GREAT QUOTES FROM ALBERT EINSTEIN

One of the benefits for me when I started working with Affirmations was that I could easily turn stressful situations around before allowing them to take over my entire day. Some of my favorites when faced with a stressful situation are: "I know that everything is working for my higher good" and, "I trust that only good comes my way" and, "I trust the process of life and life is good." Repeating these several times would dissolve any stress that I would feel rising in my body. It's all about being aware of our thoughts because our thoughts are powerful and they shape our life experiences. When we persistently think positive thoughts, we get positive experiences; when we persistently think negative thoughts, we get negative experiences. If you are unsure of what your thoughts are, get in touch with how you feel. How you feel will tell you if you are thinking negatively or positively. Make the affirmation, "I am Love, Loved, Loveable and Loving" your mantra for a few days and this is sure to shift the energy around you.

According to Abraham Maslow's teachings on the hierarchy of needs, self-esteem is the second to the top of the pyramid and self-actualization is at the top of the Pyramid. "Self-actualized people are independent of the good opinion of others." Once you build that true self-confidence within you, that's when and how you become independent of the good opinion of others. When we are independent of the good opinion of others, we make decisions differently; we make decisions based on what is in our best interest and what makes us happy. We make decisions based on what is true for us.

I have often heard the saying, "What will people think?" and this is truly how they will make a decision based on what others might think. One of the ways to overcome this is when making any decision, ask yourself if this the best choice for me and does this contribute to my happiness or does this take away from my happiness. Also ask yourself when making a decision, am I making this determination from a place of fear. If you are making a decision from a place of fear ... pause and ask yourself, how I would make this decision differently if I were choosing love instead of fear.

Love is the opposite of fear and it heals all. I really find myself challenged with this one when I'm making decisions that involve my child. As parents we are always in protection mode because that's our job, right; and in protection mode a lot of it comes from a place of fear, so I pause and ask myself is this decision based on fear or am I selecting this option from a place of pure unconditional love—sometimes when we choose love, it also involves trusting the process of life. One of the affirmations that I use is, "I release all doubt and fear!" "I trust Life and Life supports me." Also teaching your children at a very early age how to make decisions is imperative to their growing process. I remind my son all the time that when he is making a decision it needs to be what is best for him and what makes him happy, and not based on what our friends are doing nor on fearing what others might think.

Fear is an illusion of the mind, danger is real.

❧ "You can conquer almost any fear, if you will only make up your mind to do so. For remember, fear doesn't exist anywhere except in the mind."

~ DALE CARNEGIE

🕉 "Expose yourself to your deepest fear; after
that fear has no power, and the fear of
freedom shrinks and vanishes, you are free."

~ JIM MORRISON

Bad News: You're not going to fit in with everyone. Good News: The great ones never do.

Gratitude

Learning to take my gratitude to a whole new level created miracles in my life. Moving beyond just being grateful for the basic things in our life—our families, homes, food, transportation—and all of these things are important items we should be grateful for. But do we reach for something to be grateful for when things don't appear to be so great, or find something to appreciate in a stressful situation, instead of focusing on what is wrong or what is not going well for us? Look for something—even the smallest thing—and be grateful. What if we shifted our consciousness to constantly be in a state of gratitude at all times—especially when things do not appear to be so desirable. Life happens and we get stressed, frustrated and irritated.

Here is a tool to help you when things are not appearing to be so great in your world. Try placing your hand over your heart, there is life in you, you are alive, be grateful that you are alive. As you take a breath in, and breathe it out, be grateful for the breath that is flowing into your body right now. Feel the breath as it is moving through your body. Your breath is your life force, send out deep gratitude for it. This is also a great way to bring you into the present moment right here, right now. There is nothing more peaceful than fully experiencing the present moment.

Constantly being in a state of gratitude automatically dissolves negativity. We always have something to be grateful for; be conscious when you wake up, wake up in a state of gratitude and it will affect how your entire day unfolds. How we begin our day is how our day unfolds, how our day unfolds is how we live our life. When you first wake up, be in a state of gratitude, wake up with affirmations being the first thing that you practice in the mornings. When I began to utilize this, it became so much easier for me to get up out of bed and start my day. When I woke up in a state of gratitude, I wasn't thinking about how tired I might be or how much sleep I got or should have gotten. While you are in the shower send out gratitude for all the wonderful things in your life that you have to be grateful for, instead of stressing about everything that you need to accomplish for the day or deadlines that you have to meet or how rushed and busy your day is going to be. Be grateful for the warm water running through your faucets, all of the conveniences that your home offers you; be grateful for every appliance in your home that makes your life easier. Can you imagine life without these luxuries?

While you are in your car take a few moments to turn the radio off and look around to find things to be grateful for, look for the beauty in nature, be grateful that the sun is shining, or the magnificent blue sky or that the rain is watering all the beautiful plants and grass or the beautiful white snow on the ground. Send out gratitude for it being a great day. Time in your car while driving is an excellent time to do your affirmations and send out gratitude. When you arrive at work, be grateful for every co-worker that you have the pleasure to work with, be grateful for your job, your paychecks, and be grateful for all of those who support you and appreciate you at work. Be grateful for the comfortable workspace that you work in, be the person that you want all of your co-workers to be at work, supportive and appreciative. There is always something to be grateful for.

Gratitude has dissolved so many stressful situations for me. There are going to be stressful times and there are going to be painful times in all of our lives. Every challenge or obstacle that we are faced with is just an opportunity for us to grow. Here are tools to help you to better manage some of those challenges and obstacles. Feel those feeling of hurt, anger, disappointment, and frustration, but don't hold on to them and allow them to settle into your body. I'm a Yoga instructor and I have seen students in class after going into a deep stretch and being fully connected, not only feel a great release in their body, but feel an emotional release as well, and tears will flow down their face. I will gently pass them a tissue and allow them to feel and be with every feeling that may be going through all fibers of their being. Our muscles in our bodies hold on to emotions and Yoga is a wonderful time to release and let that go. This doesn't happen often in class, but in the ten years that I've been teaching it has happened at least ten times. One of the ways that I will assist the students in distressing their minds is through a guided meditation during class that takes them right into relaxation which we call savasana. A lot of times, we will do a visualization to de-stress the mind, because, as we know, the body and mind are directly connected. With this the student can often feel the release in their body as they clear the stress from their mind. I will also sometimes guide them through a meditation of intense gratitude to take their gratitude to a deeper level.

Meditation On Gratitude

As they lie on their backs I ask them to scan their bodies from their toes, all the way up to the crown of the head, relaxing every muscle using their breath, as they exhale, allowing the body to sink into the mat and become fully relaxed. Bringing their attention and awareness to their heart center, I ask them to imagine the doors to the heart center opening up as we send out deep gratitude for all of our internal organs and them functioning properly, pausing, and then focusing on the heart, as it is one of the main organs of the body. We will pause between each one to give them time to feel profound gratitude. We send out gratitude for our eyes that we see with, our ears that we hear with, the nose that we smell and breathe with, the mouth that we taste with and communicate with everyday, and the skin that allows us to feel. We are especially grateful for our arms and hands, as we think about everything they do for us each day, our legs and feet because they take us every where we want to go. We also send out gratitude for our mind that thinks thousands of thoughts daily and a special gratitude for the choice we have to be able to choose a different thought, a more peaceful thought or a happier thought. Most importantly, we send out gratitude for our breath, our breath is our life force and we feel that life force as it moves through our body.

Now I will give them some time to go down their list of things that they are grateful for, asking them to find something in nature — and to be grateful for the small things that we sometimes take for granted. After a few minutes when they are really basking in gratitude, I ask them to bring to the front of their mind one thing that is bringing stress into their world, or frustrating them or irritating them; then I ask them to find one thing about that situation or person to appreciate, something to be grateful for. If they absolutely can't find anything that they can appreciate, I ask them to just be grateful for whatever the lesson is that is in it for them. Being grateful for the lesson, even if you don't know what it is, has helped me tremendously. It's almost like the stress around the troubling situation dissolves from the body and mind.

I heard Marianne Williams say in one of her lectures that, "If we don't get the lesson it will continue to repeat itself until we do. The situation will come back around in life, it might have different characters, but it will be the same situation until we get the lesson." Wow, we have all probably experienced this at some point in our lives. Often times we don't know what the lesson is when we are in the mist of what is happening, but going to that place of being grateful for whatever the lesson might be, helps us to be open to it . We may not get it in the moment, but it will dissolve some of the negativity for us to be able to see clearer.

Being heartfelt grateful for things BEFORE they happen is a way of showing true faith.

🌀 "Gratitude opens the door to ... the power,
the wisdom, the creativity of the universe.
You open the door through gratitude."

~ DEEPAK CHOPRA

Dissolving Stress & Creating Change

🌀 "An open mind allows you to explore
and create and grow. Remember that
progress would be impossible if we always
did things the way we always have."

~ DR. WAYNE DYER

If you are looking for change in your life, you have to do something different than you have been doing to get a different result. What is your daily routine? Making small changes in your daily routine can create huge changes in your life. Gratitude and affirmations have been life changing for me. Using opportunities when you first awake in the mornings, to immediately reach for an affirmation or go to that place of gratitude, helps you to start your day on a positive note.

I teach Stress Management Workshops in the workplace and I had a Director of Operations Manager, who was very well versed in all of the material that I teach, say to me in one of the workshops, "Angela, I do the gratitude and affirmations when I wake up every morning … that is how I start my day. I spend the first five minutes before my feet hit the floor doing affirmations and being grateful, but as soon as I get in the shower it's gone and my mind is stressing about everything I have to get done at work that day." This is so natural for most people because in the shower is when they are planning their day and thinking of all that they have to do, and this is how their typical day starts. My response to her was, "take it with you into the shower, make Post-It notes (laminate them) and put them on your bathroom mirror." Post them in your shower to remind you that while you are in the shower, you are going to spend that time being grateful or doing your affirmations. "I am showered with positive thoughts all day long," is a befitting affirmation to do in the shower. "Today is a great day, I accomplish all that I need to do easily and effortlessly." "I support and appreciate those that I work with, as they support and appreciate me." "Everything I need to get through my day shows up for me easily and effortlessly." "My day is stress free, as I accomplish all that needs to be done." "I enjoy the work that I do and the people that I work with." "I embrace new opportunities every day." "I am grateful for all the good in my life." All of these are effective affirmations to do in the shower or in your car on your way to work. Choose the ones that speak to you or create your own and put these affirmations on Post-Its, then place them on your bathroom mirror, in your car, and on your computer, as a reminder.

Post them on your fridge and do affirmations while you are in the kitchen cooking. Train your mind to be in a constant state of gratitude or always have a positive affirmation going on in your mind—it will change your life. It's important to remember that stress is only the thoughts that we create around a situation and we have the choice to choose a different thought. We have the choice to replace those stressful thoughts with happier or more peaceful thoughts, reach for gratitude or one of your affirmations that you are working with.

 "There is a huge difference between wanting
to change and being willing to change.
Almost everyone wants to change for the
better. Very few are willing to take the
steps necessary to create that change."

~ JOHN T. CHILD

 "Initiate a habit of choosing thoughts
and ideas that support feeling good
and powerful, and that elevate you to
a higher level of consciousness."

~ DR. WAYNE DYER

"You are free to choose, but the choices you
make today will determine what you will do
and have in the tomorrows of your life."

~ ZIG ZIGLAR

Awaken to the Parent that You Were Meant to be and Allow Your Children to be the Child that They Are Meant to be

A very wise women once said to me, "Getting the college degrees and the job, getting married, having kids is the easy part in life, it's the other stuff that is hard, it's the mastering of life that is the difficult part." Connie is one of my Yoga students and has become a dear friend and I love the conversations that we have sometimes after class. My interpretation of what she meant by that was unlearning the learned behavior that we were taught as children, replacing the negative with positive when the negative is hardwired within us, replacing love where fear lives within us. Mastering relationships, accepting what is, to be able to live in the present moment, as a parent being able to let go of control and the need to be right—that's the difficult part!

When I learned that our belief systems and our personalities are formed by the age of 7, I knew how precious those first years of childhood are, the importance of modeling the behavior that you want your child to display—because they don't do what we say, they do what we do. They model every action and every word that comes from our mouths. I quickly realized how negative language and criticism affect everything in their being and it destroys their confidence. It is easier to build up a child than to repair an adult, and no parent wants their child to have to recover from their childhood. So I made the choice to take the words NO, DON'T, STOP, and QUIT out of my vocabulary when Javier was just a baby. Taking these negative words out of my vocabulary did not mean that my son was never told "no," he was told "no" in a positive manner. When I did this I became aware of how often we criticize and punish what we consider bad behavior, when what we could be doing is teaching appropriate behavior instead.

Our children are precious beings, why do we constantly tell them No, Don't, Stop, Quit or "because I said"? If every parent would replace those words with an explanation of why they can't do something and offer other options, our children today would display that same behavior when communicating with other children. How we communicate with our children is how they will communicate back to us, they are modeling our behavior right back to us and this is how we are teaching them to communicate with the rest of the world. I encourage you as a parent to be conscious not only of the negative words that you use but also your tone that you use with them. This can be very damaging to their self esteem. They are precious beings that are learning how to be and respond, and they are learning it directly from how they are being parented. A lot of us parent how we were parented because that is what we know; a few of us did not agree with how our parents did it, so we chose to do the opposite, but most of us are parenting our own inner child. What I mean by this is that we are parenting our children from a place of what WE did not get as a child.

Becoming a conscious parent involves parenting your child from a place of pure unconditional love, as this is what every child needs. Your child does not need what you did not get as a child, they are a totally different being and all any of them need is pure unconditional love. They especially need that when they are acting out. Most of the time when a child is acting out, there is a need that is not being met or we simply just need to validate their feelings; punishment only creates anger and animosity in them. I am not saying that there should never be consequences and life is full of natural consequences, but especially as toddlers, if we always responded and reacted to them from a place of pure unconditional love this would be their learned behavior.

I am going to share a story with you about how I experienced, and saw firsthand, the results of parenting from two different perspectives. Please don't get me wrong, Jorge is a very good father to our son Javier, but in the beginning we had different perspectives on how to parent him. When Javier was about three years old, I saw a conflict between Javier and his dad and I had never seen Javier react in this manner before. My husband had the idea that most parents behave in a certain way when it comes to correcting their kids. He thought that he should be able to look at Javier and in a very firm voice say "NO!" as he was pointing his finger, and that Javier's reaction should be that he just walks away to go do something else. Unfortunately, it just doesn't work this way. Javier would respond to him in the same tone that Jorge was using to speak to him. Javier was only modeling his dad's behavior back to him; this is what kids do and then we scold them for acting in the same manner that we, as parents, are behaving. So I said to Jorge, "Javier and I don't have the conflict that I see going on between the two of you, why don't you just try what I do. Just simply explain to him why you don't want him to do something and offer him other options of what he can do. It really is that easy." Jorge's immediate response was as most parents would be, "He needs to respect me." I said, " Absolutely he needs to respect you, but it's up to you to show him what respect looks like, it's up to you to model that for him if you want him to model it back to you. When you look at him and say NO! in a demanding voice, he is modeling that behavior right back to you. If you explain to him why he can't do something and you offer him other options, you are showing him respect, and respect is what he will model back to you. I'm just asking you to try it and see what happens." Jorge said to me, "When my dad said NO! I knew what no meant and I did not ask again." My response to that was, " you were raised from a place of fear, and it is my hope that Javier is not raised from a place of fear but rather a place of love. It is my hope that we teach him at a young age how to better communicate with us and the rest of the world because this is what we are modeling for him." I knew he walked away from that conversation a little frustrated, but in only a couple of months, Jorge looked at me with a shrug to his shoulders and said "I guess you are right".

I was relieved, as I know this is how the cycle gets broken, because we don't have to do it just like our parents did it or like everyone else is doing it. As I know that all of our parents were doing the best that they knew how. We really need to take our egos out of the parenting process; we don't always have to be right and they don't have to do it just because we said so, because that is only getting a temporary behavior from them in that moment, this is not creating long-term results. When you take the "No, Don't, Stop, Quits" out of your vocabulary, do away with your time-outs, and replace this with actually teaching appropriate behavior, that is what will bring long-term results. Javier has never been put in "Time Out"—ever. I have seen parents over and over use "Time Out" only to see the child repeat the same behavior. Time-out is very frustrating for the child and doesn't correct the behavior. Take the time to find out why the child is behaving in the manner that they are behaving in. Pay attention to what is triggering the behavior, are they just needing attention? Sometimes negative attention is better than no attention at all from a child's point of view. Most of the time when children are acting out there is a need not being met, or they may just need their feelings validated.

Outside of just needing attention there are two basic things that can easily trigger a child's behavior—sleep and eating habits. If children are not getting enough sleep they are easily irritated, therefore, they cry at the drop of a hat and then they get in trouble with their parents for acting in such a manner. All kids need a regular scheduled bedtime for adequate sleep and regular scheduled meal times with proper nutrition and sometimes a healthy snack in between. I know this sounds very basic, but I'm amazed when I see this so often not happening among some of the most educated families. Additionally, they need unconditional love—this goes a long way.

Every child is one caring adult away from being a success story.

As parents, realizing that the best relationship that you could have with your child has little to do with THEIR behavior and everything to do with YOURS—is called awareness. Being aware of how we react and respond to our children's behavior is key to getting the best results from them. Every time I react or respond to Javier in a less-than-desired manner, I ask myself ... could I have done that in a more kind and loving manner? Almost always the answer is YES, absolutely I could have. No child deserves to be screamed or yelled at. Taking this a step further lets look at the emotion that is going on within us when we react or respond in a less-than-desired way. Ask yourself, "What is it that I'm stressed about, frustrated about or what has just irritated me to cause me to react to my child's behavior in such a negative manner?" As parents, being aware and learning how to deal with the emotion inside of us, before we react to our children, is a big part of being a conscious parent. Children respond to love, love is the key to getting them to change their behavior long-term, and sometimes they just need an explanation or to be offered other options. Responding and Reacting to your child in a positive manner, praising them, lifting them up, will give them the confidence that they need in life to accomplish anything.

❧ "If we taught every 8-year-old to meditate for one year, world violence would be eliminated"

~ DALI LAMA

❧ "The example we set for our kids ... How to act when things don't go OUR way ... is much much more important than the rules we set for them."

~ LEO BABAUTA

Dedicated to Pam Retting, more than a friend, a teacher, motivator and an inspiration to me. You have always believed in me and fully supported me.

To all of my clients and students who have been so open and receptive to my work, you have contributed greatly to my growth by allowing me to share the knowledge that I've have obtained from all of my great teachers and life experiences. Special gratitude to all of my wonderful teachers and resources that are available to me. Dr. Wayne Dyer, Louise Hay, Marianne Williamson and Deepak Chopra, your work has impacted my life greatly and you inspire me every day.

~Angela Serna

My Own Eyes

"in a darkness that wasn't scary,
she glittered and intrigued me,
seeing women of the ages in
her profile. she turned her eyes
towards me. i saw my own eyes
in hers ... and the world shook."

~ TERRI ST. CLOUD
www.BoneSighArts.com

April L. Dodd

APRIL L. DODD, M.A.'s unshakable dance with possibilities grew into an accessible self-study online course called "Holy is H.I.P. & Other Spiritual Accessories for the Awakening Soul", offering transformational tips, tools, and other imperfect stories for the recovering perfectionist harboring a sacred self that's tired of hiding.

April is an inspirational speaker, Executive Coach, compassionate Life Coach, award-winning actress, and author. With a Master's in Spiritual Psychology, April serves as a trusted confidant, guide, and partner in co-creating transformational possibilities with thousands of children, professionals, and life enthusiasts. April resides in Austin, TX, creating new possibilities every day with Paul and their 2 children.

april@aprildodd.com
www.aprildodd.com

The Dance of  Possibilities

When I was recovering from the emergency cesarean that helped me give birth to my first child, I was healing, but also in excruciating pain and in terror at being a new mom. Just laughing would make me curl over in pain while my newborn unleashed a rampage on my nipples, like Jaws after a 10-day juice cleanse. I was failing at the breastfeeding thing, I was snippy with my husband, and I needed more help to take care of myself than my Type A spiritual warrior personality could bear. This entering-into-motherhood thing wasn't going to be as graceful as I had told the Universe it would.

I had imagined going in that I'd be happy being pregnant, the birth would be easy, and I'd be blissed out. I figured I'd love nursing her, lovingly accept motherhood and be totally at ease with it. I believed this perfection was possible because of all the spiritual work I had done.

What actually happened was I didn't like being pregnant, I nearly died of massive blood loss during labor, and I was on my fourth day in the hospital with a bloated body and a throbbing scar, trumped only by the searing pain in my nipples.

"I can't do this. I shouldn't be in this much pain. I am a bother to everyone. I'm too much for my busy husband. I am already failing at being a mother, therefore I am failing God." This was the way the peanut gallery of voices in my head chose to reinforce my long-held belief in my own unworthiness.

These voices weren't anything new to me. They had colored the tenor of my life since childhood when I had been immersed in an environment of taunting brothers and family dysfunction that led to painful experiences throughout my adolescence. I'd spent years pursuing therapies, workshops, and transformational programs, in an effort to quiet the negative self-talk and self-doubt that led me into heavy moods. I longed to follow the truth of my Spirit. Before my daughter's birth, I thought I had dug deep enough and put down the weight long enough to be able to lift myself through any challenges that came my way. But as prepared as I thought I was, I had merely landed on the crest of a whole new wave of inner strife.

One late evening at the hospital, after my daughter had been brought back to the nursery so I could sleep (that's a joke, you know ... you never actually *sleep* in a hospital), I set out on my next personal achievement, to go pee, all by myself.

My doula-husband Paul, who is my hero that I call Love, was reading under a buzzing florescent light on the not-so luxurious sofa, his makeshift bed for the week. I'd been bugging him all day already for favors like scratching my pinky toe, or to stop making me laugh (it's a challenge for him not to be funny), so I hated to interrupt him again. Trying to be as quiet as possible, I sat up in bed planning to swing my legs over the side of the bed without being noticed. I winced, revealing the breath I'd been holding, and Love jumped to my bedside.

"I can do it." I put my hand up.

"Oh, I know you can. I was just, you know, standing here ... doin' nothin'." He stood as if he were casually leaning against a wall, flipping a coin, waiting for the bus to arrive.

I laughed. A sharp pain ripped through my lower abdomen and I doubled over. "Don't make me laugh," I cried.

Literally, I cried. And cried. And cried some more. I realized then that this trying-to-do-things-all-by-myself maneuver was foolish and immature and left me huddled over, staring at a puddle of tears pouring onto the lap of my hospital gown. Poor guy didn't know what to do, (and it seemed I'd taken all his typical rescue tools away). I told him not to help me (Guy tool #1: fix it). I told him not to make me laugh (Guy tool #2: escape tactic). I blubbered on and on about what a terrible mother I was going to be, what have I gotten myself into, "My own mother is dying! (she was), I can't even take care of myself, and this is just impossible, I don't know how to balance all this spiritual shit with being a mom, God help me I've failed already!" (Guy tool #3: find answers or run like hell)! I had wrestled to get my baby secure on my breast and fed that day, but all I was sure the effort fed that night was my insecurities and negative beliefs.

"Love?" he said gently.

"What?" I didn't even lift my head.

"Love?"

"What?" I sobbed.

"Look at me. You've got this. And I've got you. And you've got everything you need to do this. There's no rush. I'm not going anywhere. You don't have to rush this for anyone. Ever. Take your time. I'm here all night. Two drink minimum. Tip your waitress. It just allows me more time to be with you."

Time stopped. The warmth of his words softened me. It was as if all the weight suddenly fell, and I realized that I had once again blinded myself to being loved, and to what I was capable of, as I had done so many times before.

I realized I wasn't supposed to do it all by myself. I was supposed to love myself and allow myself to be loved. Out of that love would come all the support I needed to be a great mom ... if I let it. I returned to remembering what was possible.

Paul was so patient with my impatience and his love was so strong that I was forced to realize how unworthy I had felt to receive it. I was busy rushing to be healthy, so I could be discharged to go home and be the perfect mom. But as his words entered me, a powerful shift swept through me, as gentle and sure as Paul's clear blue eyes.

I felt all the old critical voices that had bubbled up into my blubbering monologue, release. The chains that had bound me melted, and I came into a sense of internal agreement—a deep but familiar place inside myself that knew it was safe. The voices retreated gracefully into my heart, like ghosts disappearing in the light of the sunrise, and I stood in a new and childlike, vulnerable soft skin, raw with my new self. Paul held steady at my unfolding. Not just in his belief, but in his hands.

"May I have this dance?" he asked into the sacred silence that contained the room.

"What?" I lifted my head. He stepped forward, gently raised me up, and pressed me against him. His big hands wrapped around my waist and placed my other hand on his heart. He swayed ever so softly and hummed against my wet cheek.

As I rested my head against his chest, I felt as if I had been welcomed home after a long journey away, and I claimed it.

It took me fifteen minutes to walk from my bed to the bathroom, five feet away. Paul's unwavering commitment and connection inside himself helped me see the harsh judgments and misinterpretations I had held about myself. His steadfast belief in me allowed me to see that he was right, that I could do this—that I had all the inner resources necessary to deal with being a mom. That I could answer the call of motherhood, not in the way I had planned, but I could open and be able to handle any moment, one at a time with the tools I had. I saw I was a beautiful person, fully capable of being nurturing and loving, even with the added demands. I could stop putting so much pressure on myself to do it "right," whatever that was.

Up to that moment, my programming from childhood, that had me believing that I had to do things a certain way, had not been removed through my spiritual work. The idea of being "spiritual" inflated my belief in an ideal of perfection. I made it mean that I had to have all my spiritual bases covered, and always behave and feel like an enlightened angel. Perfection in my mind was not a birthright, but rather a destination, a state I needed to achieve in order to make myself right with the world, God, and as a mom.

What I failed to see was that to seek my ideal of perfection closed the doors to all possibility. If I could 'arrive' in some perfected state of humanness, then there was no room for something new. And if there was nothing new, everything was stale, old, decaying into death.

The imperfect experience that brought me into motherhood showed me that there is no place to land here. There is no final state on Earth in which to arrive at perfection because life is constantly changing. In life, there is no perfection. Only possibilities. And living in possibilities means seeing something new and being something new with whatever comes my way.

Paul's gentleness called me to return to my Self and to surrender the deep and outdated layers of expectations I had clung to, even after years of spiritual study and practice. I let them go that night and swayed into motherhood.

To My Love and all the awakenings you offer me, I could drink a case of you because you feel like home to me. To Grace and Hamilton, I love you forever, always, in all ways, no matter what. You're all my magic. My Heaven.

To the souls who came into my childhood path to help create a curriculum for me that continues to reveal my areas of growth, well done!

I will forever acknowledge my unstoppable brother, Jim, for showing me what possibility looks like.

To Richard, HATAMA.

Special thanks to Robin Colucci Hoffman.

~April L. Dodd

I Am Enough

"lifting the cover of shame and
self doubt, she dropped it on the
ground. stepping into the light
she slowly lifted her head. this
is who i am. and i am here. and
i am enough. the light warmed
her face and her heart."

~ TERRI ST. CLOUD
www.BoneSighArts.com

Brenda Fedorchuk

BRENDA FEDORCHUK is an Author, Speaker, Life Coach and Workshop Leader. As a natural leader, Brenda has devoted her life to helping others. Brenda founded Heart Centered Solutions to create a safe space for unlimited personal development through mind, body and spirit.

As a Licensed and Certified Heal Your Life® Teacher and Life Coach, Brenda teaches transformational techniques based on the philosophy of Louise Hay.

During her thirty-year career in the corporate arena, Brenda's training and experience well equipped her for success in her second career creating opportunities for individuals to step into their best life! Brenda@HeartCenteredSolutions.ca

www.Faccbook.com/HeartCenteredSolutions
www.HeartCenteredSolutions.ca

194

An Evolutionary Journey
to Authentic Power

"*The hospital is waiting for you! You have to take your son to be admitted right now!*" I held back the tears, paralyzed with fear and trying to stay calm in front of my 14-year-old son who was clearly in shock. I saw a look of complete terror in his eyes. Oh my God! *What was happening to him?*

I glanced over at my husband who gave me a look as if to say, 'We have to pull it together, as we always have, so we can be there for Jeremy.' I couldn't hold his gaze for long, for fear that we would both break down in what my kids affectionately call the *ugly cry*. I was numb. I felt sick to my stomach, terror hitting me in waves. I held my breath. I couldn't exhale. My training in the corporate world had taught me how to maintain a calm exterior even when my insides were churning. I was talking to my son, all the while holding back tears and feeling fearful for his future.

In three short hours our lives changed forever. Our son Jeremy had spent the week prior practicing for a city track meet in which he would represent his school by competing in six events. Over the week I watched his water consumption increase steadily, to the point where he was drinking a litre of water during the night. He was tired and dehydrated. I took him to his doctor for a routine check because I had a feeling something was wrong. Our family doctor took his blood glucose reading and it wouldn't read on the glucose meter. We were sent immediately to a pediatric specialist who rushed us into his office to test Jeremy's blood sugar. The specialist told us the reading was 35 mmol/L, where a normal range is between 4-7 mmol/L. The diagnosis? Type I diabetes. I was in shock, going through the motions, as we drove to the hospital, my son looking to us for answers we didn't have.

Once on the pediatric ward, the diabetic educator sat us down, as a family, and began an intensive training that lasted for two days. Looking back, I know that most of it didn't sink in. How could it? I was in shock. I slept at the hospital every night, never leaving my son's side. Reams of information were shoved at us about the dangers of Type I diabetes, its long-term effects, how insulin and carbohydrates work, what a 'low' was, how exercise affected insulin, and how to give insulin into the fat tissue and not muscle. I learned to administer Jeremy's needles by practicing on oranges and giving myself needles. I learned that a girl exactly my son's age was also in the hospital, but in a coma because of the affects of her blood glucose reading being out of range at 25 mmol/L. This was ten points less than Jeremy's. Doctors were unable to explain why my son was still walking around and not in a coma or how diabetes would affect him long-term. When I called my boss to tell him I needed time off to manage this transition, he responded with, "Really? Lots of people have diabetes. He'll be fine. Aren't you over-reacting just a little bit?"

I very quickly became aware that I would need to be an advocate for my son, given that there were broad misunderstandings of the critical differences between Type I and Type II diabetes. I found myself giving an educational presentation to the staff at his school the day after he was released from the hospital. I felt scared. Recognizing that this disease is life threatening and difficult to control, I felt fearful for his future and knew that my priorities had shifted.

My awareness grows

I knew in my heart that I wanted to change how I showed up in life and that I wanted my contributions to the world to be more meaningful. The managerial position I held in the corporate world—the one I had worked so hard to get—no longer held its alluring appeal. In that role I was unable to find the happiness I had worked so hard to find, and yet, I knew that I still needed a way to contribute to the financial welfare of my family. I felt conflicted and constricted.

Life isn't a dress rehearsal. In the mid-eighties the self-help movement was just beginning. I was reading and studying many of the self-help pioneers like Louise Hay, Tony Robbins, Wayne Dyer, and Deepak Chopra. I knew the theory well, but the practical application was difficult some days. The self-help movement was seen as very 'woo woo' and 'out there.' I had such a deep desire to do something with my life that truly mattered, and knew somehow the self-help information was related, but couldn't figure out the link between the two.

> "When we consistently suppress and distrust our intuitive knowingness, looking instead for authority, validation and approval from others, we give our personal power away."
>
> ~ SHAKTI GAWAIN

I looked outside of myself for ways to define who I was. I looked for others opinions or my corporate job to define me. I struggled with personal power; it seemed like I wanted control over my life, but didn't know how to harness true power to find true happiness. I watched others use power as a weapon, to control or to bully people, and I knew deep down inside that's not what I wanted. I searched for positive models to learn from.

When I'm thrown down, I learn to get back up again

Learning situations in life don't always present themselves in a nice box with a beautiful bow on them. Sometimes life throws you some really nasty, ugly situations that are life-altering and that force you to make a choice. We have the power to decide how we show up and manage these situations. We are the only ones responsible for our lives.

I grew up in a household where wounds were kept alive through the telling and re-telling of stories, where criticism, shame and ridicule were important to keep you "humble." *Don't get too big for your britches,* I was told. *My, my ... who do you think you are?*

I worked for and with folks in the corporate world who played favourites, marginalized their employees, and were disrespectful and mean-spirited to co-workers. *That's the way it is,* I heard. *Don't be so sensitive, grow a thicker skin, and beat them at their own game.* I didn't want to play that game and felt like a fish out of water. What could I do? Was life meant to be difficult, one big crisis after another? Was I meant to suffer? Would I ever break free and amount to anything?

My past held all of my power. It told a story about who I was, and resigned me to the role of a victim, a victim of circumstance without hope or tools to create a new future. I was familiar with daily drama, fighting, alcoholism, put-downs, teasing, mental abuse, and anger, as these were all part of my formative years and became part of my daily life. This was in addition to holding grudges, creating camps, and taking hostages by seeing who agreed with you and who didn't. Looking back, it seems I was surrounded mostly by negativity and criticism. I was convinced that if I could only change *those* people, my life would be better. This attitude left little room for creative thinking, hopes, or dreams. All of my energy was spent talking about what others were doing to me and discussing their "problems" over and over.

How do you know if YOU need to change?

Do you feel criticized? Marginalized?

Do you believe what others think of you is the truth about who you truly are?

Is what others believe about you more important than your own beliefs? Do you look to these people for external gratification?

Do you believe a better job, more money, bigger house, boat, or a new car will change your life? That these objects really mean something?

Do you carry shame for circumstances in your past, even those beyond your control?

Do you believe you will never break free from your past?

I felt this way too.

A trusted coach once asked me, "What is it that YOU want, Brenda?"

I sat there, stunned and without a clue. I had never considered what I wanted to be an option.

❧ "The soul always knows what to do to heal itself. The challenge is to silence the mind."

~ LAO TZU

Seven Tools for Daily Practice

Allow me to share with you a daily practice that has helped me find my personal power by learning about who I really am and coming to truly love myself.

🎋 "Transformation happens moment by
moment and it can happen at any time, it's
not just a declaration you make on 1 Jan."

~ BARBARA DE ANGELIS

✂ 1. What's your why? How to step up and claim your life.

Once you decide to make a change in your life, you need to know what your 'Why' is. Why are you working to make this change? Why is this important? Write your answers down so that during the difficult times you can recall why you decided to answer the call to an evolutionary life. In my case, it was the desire to evolve and create a better life. With my son's diagnosis, I saw firsthand how one's life could change in an instant. I no longer wanted to chase dreams that were not meaningful or have people or relationships in my life that were not supportive. Meet yourself where you are, without judgement, shame, or criticism. It is what it is, and you are where you are, and that's okay. Really—it's all good! Using judgement, shame, or criticism to force a change will not produce the lasting results you desire.

✂ 2. Begin by OBSERVING yourself.

What makes you happy? What drains your energy? What are you grateful for? What language and words do you use when you talk to others and/or describe situations? Notice and keep track of your observations in a journal. Remember: NO judgment or criticism.

✂ 3. Learn to LOVE and ACCEPT yourself.

Is how you treat yourself serving your highest good? Do you hold on to negative messages about yourself or a wear a label on your forehead that marginalizes and negatively defines you? Are you willing to give up these limiting beliefs and be the amazing person the world is waiting for?

Learning to love and accept yourself is about choices. Yes, you can remove that label or that obstacle keeping you from the life you truly desire. You can decide who you are by creating healthy boundaries, eating well, and exercising. You are a precious child of this universe who is here for a very important reason. I invite you to explore how great this possibility could be for you.

✂ 4. Forgiveness

This is key! Forgive every person who has hurt you and learn to forgive yourself. Forgiveness is a continual, ongoing process. Accept that people will disappoint you because people and systems are flawed. Carrying bitterness and hatred leaves you powerless by focusing your energy, thoughts and grievances on others.

> "As I walked out the door toward the gate that would lead to my freedom, I knew if I didn't leave my bitterness and hatred behind, I'd still be in prison."
>
> ~ NELSON MANDELA

✂ 5. Raise your vibration

Find inspiration that will raise your vibration. As a student and now a Heal Your Life® teacher based on the work of Louise L. Hay, I use her affirmations and teachings every day to manifest greatness in my life. One such affirmation I use a lot is as follows:

🦋 I love and approve of myself.

Out of this situation only good will come.

I am safe and all is well.

Read a piece of inspirational literature every day, even if it's just a few lines. What we focus on grows, so if we remain positive and focused on good, we will—in turn—be showered with more goodness.

Learn to meditate because through meditation you find a space containing your true, authentic self. This is a space where you will know and understand how great you truly are and that you are here to shine and be the very best person you can be. You are like a deep ocean and in the depth of that ocean is the essence of its heart. No matter what is happening on the surface, no matter how hard the wind blows or the rain pours, the ocean's deep waters remain calm and centered.

✺ 6. Create your new life

Use affirmations and visualization to create your new life. Surround yourself with like-minded friends who love you and accept you as you are. Start to visualize everything you want in your new life, whatever that may be for you. The possibilities are endless. Use humour and laughter to lighten the load.

✺ 7. Get support when you need it

I became a life coach because I believe so strongly in coaching's healing abilities. I myself had an amazing coach who gave me tools that supported my growth and development and helped me find my evolutionary path to personal power. My first coach opened up this world for me. She believed in me and taught me the rigor necessary to find my way back home to myself. She believed I had the answers within, and I did. She did this through loving kindness and support. I invite each of you to reach out and find someone you trust to lovingly support you when you need it!

My true authentic self is revealed

Every difficult situation, heartbreak, and disappointment has provided me with an opportunity to learn more about myself. This evolutionary journey was necessary to find my way back to who I truly am. Once I did, I understood that I have always been someone loveable and awesome, but I needed to polish off the dust of darkness, so that I could allow the golden light from my heart to shine through.

It's always been a knowing deep inside that I've learned to pay attention to and trust over time. Some say many are called but few answer. I know without a doubt that I have been drawn toward this evolutionary path and I clearly understand that I have answered the call to be my highest good.

Each day I make the choice to honour myself by asking these questions:

- Did I stay within my principles and values?
- Did I honour myself by living with integrity?
- Was I compassionate with myself?
- What difference did I make today?

I invite you to give yourself permission to ponder the possibilities of how great your evolutionary life can be when you reach for your highest good.

"You are built not to shrink down to less, but to blossom into more. To be more splendid. To be more extraordinary."

~ OPRAH WINFREY

Dedicated to my husband Pat, you are my best friend and my rock! Thank you for always believing in me. To my children, Amanda and Jeremy, I treasure you both with all my heart. Your love and support remain the source of my inspiration.

To all the devoted readers, my family and my friends—I am filled with such gratitude for your support and love. A special thank you to the many coaches, teachers and mentors along my path for their wisdom and guidance, especially Karen Bonner, Bob Chartier, Marianne Williamson, Cheryl Richardson, Louise Hay, Dr. Patricia Crane, and Rick Nichols.

~Brenda Fedorchuk

Darkness and Light

"her hand touched mine. darkness
and light holding each other. loving
each other. needing each other.
touching, we begin to say hello."

~ TERRI ST. CLOUD
www.BoneSighArts.com

Stars inside

"she had stars inside her, and she
knew it. she wasn't supposed
to give them away. she was
supposed to let them shine."

~ TERRI ST. CLOUD
www.BoneSighArts.com

Afterthoughts From Editor-At-Large

Now that we've read these heartfelt stories from the remarkable women authors in this book, what transformational bits of knowledge have we gleaned? Let's take a moment to reflect on some of their wisdom ... in a nutshell ... to take with you on your own personal journey:

Michelle Mullady ... *For many years I lived with a guarded heart. I desperately avoided my true feelings and the issues I'd acquired throughout my life. As I grew to love all of who I am, my world started budding in beautiful and mysterious ways. ... Learning to love yourself is the quantum leap forward that can make every area of your life better.*

Valentina Galante ... *The lessons I learned were that I needed to pay attention to my thoughts, practice self-love, eliminate drama and dysfunction in my life, and quiet my mind and outside noise, so I could hear the beautiful messages my soul and God give me every day.*

Catherine Madeira ... *It's ours, our memory (past or future) to see and use if we choose to. It's as simple as opening yourself to the tidal wave of understanding. Believe what comes to you, the more you believe the more you will be given.*

Mickey Mackaben ... *Mindful or mindless, my thoughts contribute to my intention. ... Out of not honoring that, my mind worked alone in creating this intention. It showed up in what could have been a devastating outcome. This is why it is important to bring your intention from your mind down to your heart, before it physically manifests.*

Cindy Ray ... *I began with the attitude that I had every right to blame my parents, my spouse, my kids, or anyone else I felt had wronged me. ... When I recall how peaceful I felt letting go of the blame, it reminds me that my emotions and feelings are my choice. I get to decide my level of serenity in any situation.*

Tina Gibson ... *My inner child had remained in this dungeon, while the rest of me grew up. ... Like a caterpillar emerging from its cocoon, we completed the metamorphosis. She took her rightful place in the safety of my heart, and I became whole.*

Kourtney Hall ... *When I think of awakening and creating happiness, love, success, prosperity, and esteem for myself, I know it has to start from what I am sending out to the universe. How I send messages out to the universe is through energy, and how I create that energy is through my thoughts. Love yourself, and be kind to yourself. Treat yourself as you would your close friend.*

Tauri Hall ... *I have learned the damage of clinging, hanging on so tight in order to feel safe, when in reality, it put me at risk. ... I learned to turn around and offer myself what I thought I so desperately needed from others—love, security, approval, acceptance, and commitment. I learned to take myself by the hand and not let go.*

Deanna Leigh ... *Being open allows everyone the freedom to hear what needs to be heard, to change what needs to be changed, and to awaken what needs to awaken. ... Your awakening will come from a deep place and you will emerge into a beautiful butterfly! That is when your purpose will soar.*

Verity Dawson ... *For myself, I learned that my spirituality was integral to who I was as a person; that no matter what was going on around me, if I kept my inner peace, I was transformed from an Alice in Wonderland, where rare events overtook her, to Wonder Woman where everything had a place and a reason.*

Kisty Stephens ... *It was that day I learned to be happy where I was, with what I had. I may have been broken, but I had to break wide open to let the light into my heart. ... The Sparrows taught me to be faithful to the* moment, respect everyone, especially those I don't understand, and above all be gentle and kind to myself.

Constance Mollerstuen ... *When you live your life on auto-pilot, the speed with which you travel is predetermined. ... Loving yourself enough to respect your inner guidance and discover what your true purpose and calling in life is can be accomplished by taking the time to slow down and nurture yourself.*

Diana S. Christie ... *I knew that words had no meaning until I chose the meaning. I am accountable for my thoughts and actions. ... I changed my relationship with fear right then. ... As long as I am alive, the awakening is ongoing. 'I am willing to change' is my mantra.*

Angela Serna ... *When I learned to give up the need for others' approval, and learned how to love and accept myself exactly as I was, this is where I found MYSELF, this is where true happiness comes from—"within."*

April L. Dodd ... *I realized I wasn't supposed to do it all by myself. I was supposed to love myself and allow myself to be loved. ... What I failed to see was that to seek my ideal of perfection closed the doors to all possibility.*

Brenda Fedorchuk ... *Sometimes life throws you some really nasty, ugly situations that are life-altering and that force you to make a choice. We have the power to decide how we show up and manage these situations. We are the only ones responsible for our lives.*

Everyone has a different way of experiencing things that lead to their own understanding of what it means to AWAKEN. Personally, my awakening came in 1985, when those "cosmic tumblers" of movie fame started falling into place, and the Universe miraculously popped open. It was then, at the age of 40, that I made the conscious decision to start paying attention.

In the movie 'Field of Dreams," Ray Kinsella (Kevin Costner) quotes author Terence Mann (James Earl Jones) as saying: ***"There comes a time when all the cosmic tumblers have clicked into place—and the universe opens itself up for a few seconds to show you what's possible."*** Terence Mann then laments the tragic fact that most folks aren't even aware of that opening when it occurs, so they never walk through the doors that will lead them into their life's potential.

After a difficult marriage, and the resulting divorce from a bipolar alcoholic in 1985, I finally began a more introspective approach to the way I was choosing to live. The first 'cosmic portal' that 'appeared' for me was Adult Children of Alcoholics studies (my dad was an alcoholic), along with several other psychology-oriented classes and workshops. Next, I was inspired to take courses based on Ernest Holmes' remarkable philosophy book, *"The Science of Mind"* (1938), and from there I continued on into ministerial school.

In 1991 an extensive series of 'coincidences' and synchronistic happenings, created an incredible shift which catapulted me onto a path that would give my world an entirely new dimension and depth. I was suddenly and mysteriously impelled to take a leap of faith by quitting my secure and rewarding job in California and moving to Santa Fe, New Mexico, (where I knew no one) ... to give something back to the world.

" ... I unknowingly embarked on a spiritual journey that continues to this day. The cosmic tumblers turned and clicked with the precision of a finely produced Swiss chronometer. A door was unlocked, a portal was created, and the universe opened. The potential for unimaginable opportunities was made available, and amazingly, it was intended for me."

~ JOE ALONZO,
"SPIRITUAL CALLING–NURSING YOUR
PATH, NURTURING YOUR DESTINY"

I left a successful career in the Los Angeles area, leased out my house with everything in it, and moved to Santa Fe, New Mexico. As time went on, the tenants moved from my house, and I was told that the declining California real estate market made the property "unsellable." Persistent fears of whether my bank account could hold out longer than it would take my house to sell were almost overwhelming.

Battling a string of sleepless nights, I finally discovered a fear-relief formula that worked. I envisioned every aspect of how it would look, feel, smell, taste and sound for my house to sell. I "heard" the realtor's voice over the phone telling me we had an offer; I "saw" myself flying to California; I heard and saw the buyers as we did a final walk-through; I felt the check in my hand; I smelled the exhaust of the yellow rental truck after we loaded up my stuff; I tasted the teriyaki celebration dinner at a local restaurant; and I saw myself being fully immersed in my motivational project in Santa Fe with no distracting ties elsewhere.

The house went on the market October 4, 1992. There was just one offer, submitted on October 22nd (for almost the asking price), and escrow closed December 4th. It was the ONLY house my realtor sold that month. She said she knew it would happen though, because she could feel my belief in it.

"Fear is the cheapest room in the house. I would like to see you living in better conditions."

~ GREAT SUFI MASTER HAFIZ (1320-1389)

Once settled in town, I walked through every door that opened and soon, almost magically, established a holistic center called Lightship of Santa Fe, which became the first and only metaphysical organization ever to be endorsed by the city government. I also published a monthly motivational news magazine that was distributed nationally and at the Santa Fe Visitor's Bureau. The project ran from 1992-1996 and touched thousands of lives. The following poem explains my journey and practically wrote itself, as it flowed through my consciousness and out of my fingers onto the keyboard:

"Santa Fe"

Snow fell on the adobe, the air was chilled with frost,
I'd made the trek to Santa Fe, abandoning all cost.
It wasn't due to boredom or discontent I'd gone,
'Twas spiritual evolvement, a purpose yet undone.

Why I'd quit my bubble of security and friends
Was a matter of intention, to inspire a Cosmic Spin.
My head succumbed to heart-sense as I shifted into Soul,
Creating the allowance in which miracles unfold.

Gifts showed up at every turn, the picture became clear,
Pieces slipped in place with ease, I only had to "hear."
The choice to step out fearlessly and trust the Truth that IS,
Encouraged and impelled me to keep following my Bliss.

En route I faced a snowstorm, another chance to know
That fear is but illusion, we're safe within the Flow;
As I surrendered and released, inner peace returned,
Spirit took the wheel again ... the metaphor re-learned.

When I arrived in Santa Fe, I felt embraced yet free,
Surrounded by an atmosphere of sacred energy.
Artistic in its beauty, historic in its span,
A consciousness of Oneness to perpetuate The Plan.

Two weeks in town I asked myself, "Why haven't I done more?"
The Voice Within reminded me what I'd moved here for;
My worth lies not in doing, it's BEING that's my task,
Bringing in the Light We Are is why we're on The Path.

At first the nights were lonely, a time to be with me,
The Essence of my spirit was bursting from its seed;
The stars seemed so much brighter, a kinship and a bond,
A link in space to all I AM ... and destinies beyond.

Magical occurrences enraptured and amazed,
I never knew the outcome until I turned the page;
No predicting and dissecting details by degree,
My focus now was centered, revealing Me to me.

Days of insight brought me keys for opening up my heart;
Unlocking portals in the walls that kept me set apart.
Distance is still distance when I give but don't receive,
Separation's not the answer, it's vulnerability.

©Chelle Thompson, 1991

Now, in closing, let us receive another gift. This time in the form of a vivid meditative journey to solidify our newfound awareness. Our Compiler, Lisa Hardwick-Peplow, leads us on a magical journey in her Awaken Guided Meditation as: *You take the final flower and place it in your bouquet ...*

Awaken
🌿 Guided Meditation

First, take a moment to settle down, relax. Find a comfortable position. Begin to focus on your breath.

Breathe in through your nose ... Hold it a moment.

And out through your mouth ... releasing all of your breath, emptying your lungs completely.

Inhale ...

Exhale ...

Now, imagine yourself at the base of a mountain.

...

Walking down the mountain there is man. You notice that he is dressed in a white cloak. You know that you are supposed to meet this person.

As he reaches out you take his hand in yours ... He smiles, and nods. You begin to go up the mountain with your guide.

As you climb the mountain together, in his soothing voice, he explains that the path is derived from switchbacks. He says that switchbacks are trails, zigzagging back and forth all over the width of the mountain, all the way up until the path reaches the top.

You and your guide make your way to the end of the first switchback, where you find a clearing. On the ground in the center of this clearing, you notice a beautiful red flower.

You can smell its fragrance. You breathe it in and it is wonderful, magnificent. You look to your guide and notice his smile, warm and encouraging.

Your guide then explains:

The flower is for you, he says, to take on your journey. He encourages you to go over and pick up the flower, to fully breathe in its scent.

You pick the beautiful, red flower and study it for quite some time, noticing its delicate petals, its strong, thick stem, and the intoxicating smell … As you take all of this in, your guide explains the meaning:

Red is a color of action. Red awakens us, moves us and guides us toward change. Red is also the color of passion and righteous anger. It represents revolution, movement and progress.

You appreciate the words and wisdom of your guide, and reach out to take his outstretched hand in yours, once more, as you make your way back across and farther up the mountain.

Now you can feel the moist, cool air on your face. You notice that you are more relaxed and energetic as you go further along the path.

At the end of this part of the trail, you finally see something else: an orange flower in the middle of another clearing. You are still holding your guide's hand; but now you release it and walk up to the flower, knowing it is for you. You kneel and pick it up. You place this orange flower along with the red one.

You study the orange flower closely and, meanwhile, your guide explains its significance:

The color *orange* exhibits a highly spiritual energy. It transforms more delicate energy into energy your own body can use. Orange raises your awareness of the thin line that separates the physical from the spiritual.

You thank your guide for this valuable information, then recall past experiences you have had with this other side, signs you have seen in nature and life, and the meaning that links one event to the next.

You rise up and take your guide's hand once more, then start to make your way up and across the mountain. As you ascend you can sense the knowledge you have gained filling you up; it is both exciting and satisfying.

Once you reach the next clearing, you quickly look toward the center, knowing already that something awaits you.

And there it is … a beautiful, bright yellow flower. You walk over and pick it up. You stroke its petals and at once take in the lovely fragrance … Breathing in deep, you tilt your head back and up toward the sky, with a great smile on your face. You look over at your guide and see that he is smiling, too, with that same warm smile from before. He says:

Yellow indicates intuitive "knowing." It is the development of your true self, the "being" as you were created and meant to be before society told you something different.

You *know* who you were created to be. And you have always known. With this knowledge, you realize the significance of the yellow flower, the importance of its message … And so you make a promise to yourself, to take special care of the "being" you were created to be. To surround yourself with those you resonate with, and to do those things that bring you most joy. This is how you honor yourself: by being in tune with your own sense of happiness.

You continue on the path with your guide, walking up the mountain and across, closer to the next clearing.

Then you look to your guide. You meet his crystal blue eyes and give him a smile of gratitude for all his wisdom. He closes his eyes, slightly, and nods as if he knows what you are feeling. You both look ahead now … the clearing is not far. You approach the entrance and notice a flower, with green petals, growing out of the ground in the center space. You go to greet the flower, wondering if you have ever before seen such a flower with green petals.

You kneel to pluck it from the ground, bringing it closer for inspection. It is beautiful: the petals richly green and smooth. The scent is fresh, invigorating, inviting.

Your guide begins:

Green is the power of love. Green contains a teaching energy, grounding us in compassion, self-love, and the sense that we are a part of something much larger than ourselves. Green reminds us that our love and learning in life develops through relationships—with ourselves and with others.

You dwell on some of your relationships ... how you have loved and learned from each one. You realize, at this moment, the importance of such relationships in your life; relationships with others and the relationship with yourself. You breathe in the green flower's fragrance and step away from the clearing. You tuck this flower in with your bunch of flowers, and grasp them in one hand while reaching out for your guide.

You make your way to the west, again, upward and across the mountain.

You expect the next clearing at the path's end, to see it there, waiting for you ... and yet it is not. At the trail's end, your guide looks up. You follow his gaze and see a low wall in the mountain face, about six feet high, with a possible landing beyond. Your guide jumps onto the landing, deftly holds the edge of the small precipice, and pulls his body up. He immediately turns and, lying flat on his stomach, reaches for you. You take his hand and he pulls you up, easily, to where you land beside him.

It is another clearing. And standing there you look out over a valley. It is so beautiful: the quilted patches of farmland lay in the distance; to the north, there is a small town made of browns and greys and colors of the earth. And—yes—that is a small plane flying overhead, even higher than you are now. You begin to understand how high up you are, and yet you feel quite safe, enjoying the delight of this journey and discovery. With this thought, you remember the flower.

And there it is, behind you ... exactly in the middle of the clearing. It is a brilliant blue flower, just as bright and beautiful as the others. It has many long petals. You go, bend, and pick it up. The sense of awe is almost overwhelming. The stem and the weight of it in your hand ... its fragrance tickling your nose. You look at your guide and he speaks:

The color *blue* is your creativity. It is your expression, communication and connection with the Spirit. Blue is the expression of the divine within the deepest part of yourself. It represents this knowledge, that we live in such truth and are aware that each of us has a wise, inner being. You may call to this being and visit this place as often as you wish.

"Now take my hand," says your guide. There is one last path until we reach the top.

You take your guide's hand and follow him. As you approach the end of that final path, you look up to the largest of all the clearings. You are at the very top of the mountain. You walk into the center and turn around, take in the view. It is beautiful. See it. Breathe it in.

What do you see?

...

How does it feel?

...

You turn around for your flower. There it is: where you knew it would be—at the clearing's center. The flower is gorgeous, indigo in color. You pick it up and inspect it. With the other flowers, in this small bouquet that you have gathered yourself, it looks even more wonderful.

Your guide explains:

Indigo represents profound wisdom and sight that extends inward and outward. It represents the moment in which you begin to identify the motions of Spirit, becoming unified with the Divine.

You take a deep breath, sensing that this knowledge and this awareness, like a lush euphoria, are one thing. You try to hold it in ... and let it out, like breath. You have felt this before, this Spirit, in your life. You promise yourself to take the time to experience it more often.

Now, you take the hand of your guide. He helps you down the mountain: and as you pass each clearing you see a new flower is growing from each center space. The stem is just five inches long, and the budding flower is small, tight, only hinting at the color inside.

You know that these flowers will be there for the next person on his or her own journey. You smile, knowing that enlightenment awaits him or her.

You arrive at the base of the mountain with your guide. You turn around to watch him come down the last part of the path. In his hand … you notice he carries *another* flower. It is a vibrant purple, the most beautiful of all the flowers you have seen. You look at his face, into his eyes, and he smiles, holding it out for you.

"Here," he says, "This is your last flower … " and then explains:

In *violet* there is the importance of Letting Go and Wholeness. Letting go of judgment, of thoughts, of things that do not serve our highest good, of utilizing all the energies and colors to AWAKEN us to Wholeness.

You take the final flower and place it in your bouquet. Remember all you have learned. You thank your guide and you embrace. It is a sweet, loving embrace. And then he turns, walking away and back up the mountain, until he is no longer there. Now you have a newfound awareness. You are able to visit this mountain and come to this place within yourself whenever you wish to AWAKEN.

~Lisa Hardwick-Peplow

Forever Changed

"maybe some things need to
be seen before you know that
they're there. but once seen,
they are easily felt. and once
felt, you are forever changed."

~ TERRI ST. CLOUD
www.BoneSighArts.com

 Resources

The following list of resources are for the national headquarters; search in your yellow pages under "Community Services" for your local resource agencies and support groups.

AIDS

CDC National AIDS Hotline
(800) 342-2437

ALCOHOL ABUSE

Al-Anon Family Group Headquarters
1600 Corporate Landing Parkway
Virginia Beach, VA 23454-5617
(888) 4AL-ANON
www.al-anon.alateen.org

Alcoholics Anonymous (AA)
General Service Office
475 Riverside Dr., 11th Floor
New York, NY 10115
(212) 870-3400
www.alcoholics-anonymous.org

Children of Alcoholics Foundation
164 W. 74th Street
New York, NY 10023
(800) 359-COAF
www.coaf.org

Mothers Against Drunk Driving
MADD
P.O. Box 541688
Dallas, TX 75354
(800) GET-MADD
www.madd.org

National Association of Children of Alcoholics (NACoA)
11426 Rockville Pike, #100
Rockville, MD 20852
(888) 554-2627
www.nacoa.net

Women for Sobriety
P.O. Box 618
Quartertown, PA 18951
(215) 536-8026
www.womenforsobriety.org

CHILDREN'S RESOURCES

Child Molestation

ChildHelp USA/Child Abuse Hotline
15757 N. 78th St.
Scottsdale, AZ 85260
(800) 422-4453
www.childhelpusa.org

Prevent Child Abuse America
200 South Michigan Avenue, 17th Floor
Chicago, IL 60604
(312) 663-3520
www.preventchildabuse.org

Crisis Intervention

Girls and Boys Town National Hotline
(800) 448-3000

www.boystown.org

Children's Advocacy Center of East Central Illinois
*(If your heart feels directed to make a donation to this center,
please include Lisa Hardwick's name in the memo)*
616 6th Street
Charleston, IL 61920
(217) 345-8250
http://caceci.org

Children of the Night
14530 Sylvan St.
Van Nuys, CA 91411
(800) 551-1300
www.childrenofthenight.org

National Children's Advocacy Center
210 Pratt Avenue
Huntsville, AL 35801
(256) 533-KIDS (5437)
www.nationalcac.org

Co-Dependency

Co-Dependents Anonymous
P.O. Box 33577
Phoenix, AZ 85067
(602) 277-7991
www.codependents.org

Suicide, Death, Grief

AARP Grief and Loss Programs
(800) 424-3410
www.aarp.org/griefandloss

Grief Recovery Institute
P.O. Box 6061-382
Sherman Oaks, CA 91413
(818) 907-9600
www.grief-recovery.com

Suicide Awareness Voices of Education
Minneapolis, MN 55424
(952) 946-7998
Suicide National Hotline
(800) 784-2433

DOMESTIC VIOLENCE

National Coalition Against Domestic Violence
P.O. Box 18749
Denver, CO 80218
(303) 831-9251
www.ncadv.org

National Domestic Violence Hotline
P.O. Box 161810
Austin, TX 78716
(800) 799-SAFE
www.ndvh.org

DRUG ABUSE

Cocaine Anonymous National Referral Line
(800) 347-8998
National Helpline of Phoenix House
(800) COCAINE
www.drughelp.org

National Institute of Drug Abuse
(NIDA)
6001 Executive Blvd., Room 5213,
Bethesda, MD 20892-9561, Parklawn
Building
Info: (301) 443-6245
Help: (800) 662-4357
www.nida.nih.gov

EATING DISORDERS

Overeaters Anonymous
National Office
P.O. Box 44020
Rio Rancho, NM 87174-4020
(505) 891-2664
www.overeatersanonymous.org

GAMBLING

Gamblers Anonymous
International Service Office
P.O. Box 17173
Los Angeles, CA 90017
(213) 386-8789
www.gamblersanonymous.org

HEALTH ISSUES

American Chronic Pain Association
P.O. Box 850
Rocklin, CA 95677
(916) 632-0922
www.theacpa.org

American Holistic Health Association
P.O. Box 17400
Anaheim, CA 92817
(714) 779-6152
www.ahha.org

The Chopra Center at La Costa Resort and Spa Deepak Chopra, M.D.
2013 Costa Del Mar
Carlsbad, CA 92009
(760) 494-1600
www.chopra.com

The Mind-Body Medical Institute
110 Francis St., Ste. 1A
Boston, MA 02215
(617) 632-9530 Ext. 1
www.mbmi.org

National Health Information Center
P.O. Box 1133
Washington, DC 20013-1133
(800) 336-4797
www.health.gov/NHIC

Preventive Medicine Research Institute
Dean Ornish, M.D.
900 Brideway, Ste 2
Sausalito, CA 94965
(415) 332-2525
www.pmri.org

MENTAL HEALTH

American Psychiatric Association of America
1400 K St. NW
Washington, DC 20005
(888) 357-7924
www.psych.org

Anxiety Disorders Association of America
11900 Parklawn Dr., Ste. 100
Rockville, MD 20852
(310) 231-9350
www.adaa.org

The Help Center of the American Psychological Association
(800) 964-2000
www.helping.apa.org

National Center for Post Traumatic Stress Disorder
(802) 296-5132
www.ncptsd.org

4444444444

National Alliance for the Mentally Ill
2107 Wilson Blvd., Ste. 300
Arlington, VA 22201
(800) 950-6264
www.nami.org

National Depressive and Manic-Depressive Association
730 N. Franklin St., Ste. 501
Chicago, IL 60610
(800) 826-3632
www.ndmda.org

National Institute of Mental Health
6001 Executive Blvd.
Room 81884, MSC 9663
Bethesda, MD 20892
(301) 443-4513
www.nimh.nih.gov

SEX ISSUES

Rape, Abuse and Incest
National Network
(800) 656-4673
www.rainn.org

National Council on Sexual Addiction and Compulsivity
P.O. Box 725544
Atlanta, GA 31139
(770) 541-9912
www.ncsac.org

SMOKING

Nicotine Anonymous World Services
419 Main St., PMB #370
Huntington Beach, CA 92648
(415) 750-0328
www.nicotine-anonymous.org

STRESS ISSUES

The Biofeedback & Psychophysiology Clinic
The Menninger Clinic
P.O. Box 829
Topeka, KS 66601-0829
(800) 351-9058
www.menninger.edu

New York Open Center
83 Spring St.
New York, NY 10012
(212) 219-2527
www.opencenter.org

The Stress Reduction Clinic Center for Mindfulness
University of Massachusetts
Medical Center
55 Lake Ave., North
Worcester, MA 01655
(508) 856-2656

TEEN

Al-Anon/Alateen
1600 Corporate Landing Parkway
Virginia Beach, VA 23454-5617
(888) 425-2666
www.al-anon.alateen.org

Planned Parenthood
810 Seventh Ave.
New York, NY 10019
(800) 230-PLAN
www.plannedparenthood.org

Hotlines for Teenagers
Girls and Boys Town National Hotline
(800) 448-3000

ChildHelp National Child Abuse Hotline
(800) 422-4453

Just for Kids Hotline
(888) 594-KIDS

National Child Abuse Hotline
(800) 792-5200

National Runaway Hotline
(800) 621-4000

National Youth Crisis Hotline
(800)-HIT-HOME

Suicide Prevention Hotline
(800) 827-7571

 A Call For Authors

Most people have a story that needs to be shared—could you be one of the contributing authors to be featured in an upcoming compilation book?

Visionary Insight Press is leading the industry in compilation book publishing. They represent some of today's most inspirational teachers, healers and spiritual leaders.

Their commitment is to assist this planet we call "home" to be a place of kindness, peace and love. One of the ways they fulfill this commitment is by assisting others in the sharing of their inspiring stories and words of wisdom.

We look forward to hearing from you.

Please visit us at

www.visionaryinsightpress.com

CPSIA information can be obtained at www.ICGtesting.com
Printed in the USA
LVOW06s2116270915

455945LV00001B/5/P